# MINOR PROPHETS OF ISRAEL

## A SELF-STUDY GUIDE

# Irving L. Jensen

**MOODY PRESS**

CHICAGO

© 1975 by
THE MOODY BIBLE INSTITUTE
OF CHICAGO

All rights reserved. No part of this book may be reproduced in any form without permission in writing from the publisher, except in the case of brief quotations embodied in critical articles or reviews.

Scripture quotations, unless noted otherwise, are from the King James Version.

The use of selected references from various versions of the Bible in this publication does not necessarily imply publisher endorsement of the version in its entirety.

Cover photo: Looking west from the Church of the Nativity in Bethlehem

ISBN: 0-8024-4480-6

3 5 7 9 10 8 6 4 2

*Printed in the United States of America*

# Contents

# Introduction

The Scriptures studied in the lessons of this manual are the books of Jonah, Amos, and Hosea. The spiritual applications intended by the books are as modern as they can be. In fact, someone has said concerning Amos that he "proclaimed a message so far ahead of his time that most of the human race, and a large part of all Christendom, have not yet caught up with it." The Bible that Jesus and the early apostles studied and taught was even then an ancient book, and yet they applied it as a timeless book (2 Tim. 3:16-17). This is how we will want to approach the very same Scriptures in the studies of this manual.

*Suggestions for Study*

Here are some suggestions for making your study of these minor prophets most effective:

1. Approach each lesson with the desire to learn what God has for you in the Bible text. Begin each study in prayer and ask the Holy Spirit to be your Teacher.

2. Spend most of your time in the Bible text itself. This study guide continually directs you to the Scriptures, mainly the text of the three minor prophets but also passages of other Bible books.

3. Train your eyes to *see* what the Bible says.

4. Use pencil or pen continually in your study. This cannot be overemphasized. Record observations, including answers to the questions of the manual and the completion of work sheets.

5. Mark paragraph divisions clearly in your Bible before you begin your analysis of each passage. This is important.

6. If you are using the King James Version as your basic study text, refer to at least one or two contemporary versions for comparative purposes. Such aids are helpful for unclear passages. All Bible quotes in this study guide are from the King James Version,

unless otherwise stated. A highly recommended modern translation is the *New American Standard Bible* (NASB).

7. Refer to commentaries only after you have completed your analysis of a particular part of the passage. The Notes section at the end of each lesson gives information concerning the Scripture passage that is not afforded by the text itself.

8. Study carefully the charts of each lesson. These will help you see more things in the passage being analyzed.

9. Try to relate the messages of the prophets to the New Testament as much as possible. For example, backsliding in the book of Hosea may be likened to falling out of fellowship with Christ (cf. John 6:66-67; Rev. 2:4-5).

## Suggestions to Group Leaders

1. *Length of study units.* There are thirteen lessons in this manual, but it is advisable to break up some lessons into smaller units because of their length. As leader of the class, you should decide before the following meeting how much of the lesson should be studied as homework.

2. *Homework.* Urge each member of the class to complete the analysis suggestions of the manual before coming to class. It is important that each member think and study for himself so that he can weigh more accurately what someone else says about a Bible text. Encourage the class to bring questions about the text to the class hour for discussion.

3. *Class participation.* Encourage all members to participate orally in the class, but do not pressure anyone to do so. Also, don't ever embarrass a person by underestimating the significance of an answer he gives or a question he asks. Concerning his answer, he often has in mind *more* than he can put in words. Concerning questions, it is a healthy sign of mental activity when questions are asked, regardless of the kind. It is true that Bible teaching comes alive in an environment of asking questions.

4. *The class hour.* Here are some practical hints:

(a) Open the class session on time, with brief, heartfelt prayer.

(b) Keep the entire meeting informal. It is not intended to be a formal worship service.

(c) Devote the opening minutes to welcoming visitors, reviewing the previous lesson, and identifying the goals of the present discussion.

(d) Devote most of the hour to a free, informal discussion of the main parts of the lesson. Illustrate the Bible passages from your own experience and encourage the members of the class to do the same.

(e) As you approach the end of the meeting, summarize the things learned and let the members suggest ways to apply the Bible truths.

(f) Make clear what the homework is for the next meeting.

(g) Close the meeting on time. Further discussion sought by members should be kept separate from the stated class meeting hour.

# Lesson 1
# The Twelve Minor Prophets

The best way to begin studying the minor prophets is to learn about their original writings. These books were not written in a vacuum—there were urgent situations in the lives of God's people with which He wanted to deal. And so at various times God called upon certain of His prophets to deliver the "Thus saith the Lord" to His people. In this lesson we will spend most of our time studying the general setting of *all* Old Testament prophecy as we relate the minor prophets to this.

## I. THE TWELVE MINOR PROPHETS

Young children memorizing the books of the Old Testament usually have an exciting time when they reach the minor prophets, because the pronunciations and rhythms are such a challenge for recitation. This is the list:

| | |
|---|---|
| 1. Hosea | 7. Nahum |
| 2. Joel | 8. Habakkuk |
| 3. Amos | 9. Zephaniah |
| 4. Obadiah | 10. Haggai |
| 5. Jonah | 11. Zechariah |
| 6. Micah | 12. Malachi |

### A. Titles

The common title for these books is "minor prophets." This title originated in Augustine's time (late fourth century A.D.). The books are "minor" only in the sense of being much shorter than such prophecies as Isaiah and Jeremiah (called "major prophets"). Their message is surely not less important today, nor was it when

7

first delivered in Old Testament times. They were minor prophets preaching a major message.

The Hebrew Bible regards these writings as one book and calls them simply "The Twelve." It was because of the books' brevity that the Jews in Old Testament times joined the twelve writings together into one scroll, so that the combined length was about the same as that of Isaiah or Jeremiah. Hence it was natural to consider them as one book, *The Twelve*.[1] At least the title is not misleading, as "minor prophets" can be.

### B. Canon

The twelve minor prophets have never been strongly challenged as being part of the inspired canon of Scripture. Their messages are just as lofty and unique as those of the major prophets and have been recognized as such.

As noted above, in the Hebrew Bible (Law, Prophets, Writings) *The Twelve* is listed as just one book of the Prophets section. This partly explains why the Hebrew Bible has a total of only twenty-four books, although those twenty-four are the exact equivalent of our thirty-nine. In the English Bible the minor prophets compose twelve of the seventeen prophetic books.

### C. Order of the List

Read again the list of the minor prophets given earlier in the lesson. It is not fully known what originally determined the order of this list. There is a general chronological pattern, in that the first six books were written before the last six. This observation is based on the order of prophets as shown on Chart B.

## II. WHY PROPHETS?

### A. A Prophet's Ministry

The ministry of prophet is an important one in the Bible. This is shown by the fact that the word "prophet" in its various forms appears more than 660 times in the Bible, two-thirds of which are in the Old Testament. The sixteen prophets who wrote the seventeen Old Testament prophetic books[2] lived over a span of about

---

1. The following second-century B.C. nonbiblical reference shows that the books were so designated before the time of Christ: "And of the Twelve Prophets may the bones flourish again from their place, for they comforted Jacob and redeemed them by assurance of hope" (Ecclesiasticus 49:10).
2. Jeremiah wrote two of the seventeen books: Jeremiah and Lamentations.

420 years. We may well ask, "Why did God raise up prophets in Old Testament times?" To answer this, we need to know what the prophetic ministry was. Gleason Archer says that the prophet (Heb., *nabi*) was "one called by God to proclaim as a herald from the court of heaven the message to be transmitted from God to man."[3] He was a combination preacher, herald, teacher, spokesman, intercessor, reformer, and even shepherd (Isa. 40:1-2). The prophet was also the moral conscience of the people, exposing and rebuking their sins (Isa. 58:1; Ezek. 22:2; 43:10; Mic. 3:8).

A prophet was primarily a spokesman for God. In Exodus 7:1 Aaron, Moses' brother, is called a prophet (the same Hebrew word *nabi* cited above). Read Exodus 4:14-16 and note how Aaron was to speak in behalf of God. Also read Jeremiah 1:4-10 to see what was involved in the typical divine commission of a prophet.

The message that the prophets delivered from God to the people involved the past, the present, or the future. If it was past or present, the prophet was *forthtelling*. If it was future, he was *foretelling*. It is interesting that we usually identify the future with prophecy, but most of the prophets' messages were of the forth-telling kind (e.g., teaching and rebuking).

All the prophetic words of the Old Testament could probably be compiled under the following four large areas of truth:

1. *Instruction of the great truths about God and man.* The prophets devoted much time telling the people about God—His character, His domain, His purpose, and His law. They also gave a true diagnosis of the spiritual health of the nations as a whole and of individual souls.

2. *Warning and appeal to those living in sin.* It cannot be said that God brings judgment upon men without forewarning. Over and over again the prophets warned of righteous judgment for sin, and exhorted the people to repent and turn to God.

3. *Comfort and exhortation to those trusting and obeying God.* These are the warm and bright portions of the prophets' messages.

4. *Prediction of events to come.* Prophetic predictions were of two major subjects: (a) national and international events, of both near and far-distant future; and (b) the comings of Jesus the Messiah—His first and second.

So an answer to the question, "Why prophets?" would be that God wanted them to be channels of revelation to man about Him-

---

3. Gleason L. Archer, *A Survey of Old Testament Introduction*, p. 284. In the New Testament there are mainly two different Greek words translated by the one English word "preach." They are *evangelizo* ("preach the good news," e.g., Luke 4:43), and *kerusso* ("proclaim," e.g., Matt. 10:27). The latter word is similar to the Hebrew root of *nabi.*

# THE WRITING PROPHETS IN OLD TESTAMENT HISTORY

Chart A

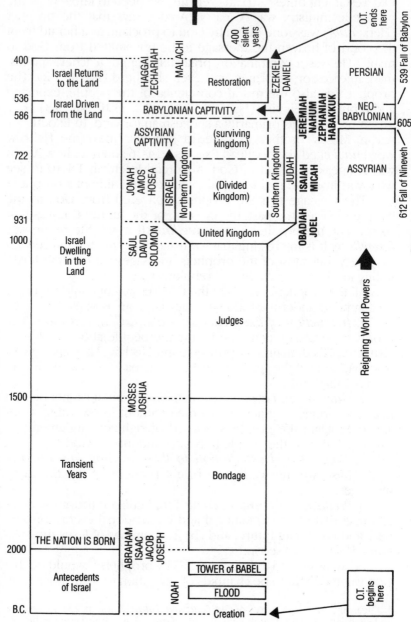

self and His will, to lead them into a vital relationship with Himself.

## B. A Prophet's Audience

We have looked briefly at *what* the ministry of an Old Testament prophet was. Now let us focus on the *who*. In particular, who was the audience of the prophet?

1. First, study Chart A carefully to get an overall view of Old Testament history. Note the following:

(a) The chosen nation of Israel came into being during the lifetime of Abraham, around 2000 B.C. (Memorize the time periods on the chart, and you will find that the many details of Old Testament history will fall into place.)

(b) Then followed a period of bondage (in Egypt) and of judges (in Canaan).

(c) A united kingdom arose in 1000 B.C. The people had demanded of God a king like those of pagan nations, to replace the judges (1 Sam. 8:4-9).

(d) The kingdom was officially split in 931 B.C.[4] The ten tribes living in the north (New Testament areas of Samaria and Galilee) seceded from the south and retained the name *Israel*. They are referred to as the Northern Kingdom. Their rivals were the two tribes living in south Canaan, known as the Southern Kingdom, or Judah.

(e) Then came the captivities. God judged Israel's sins by allowing Assyria to conquer it in 722 B.C. Judah fell to the Babylonians in 586 B.C., for the same reason.

(f) At last there was restoration. After a period of captivity, the Jews in exile (Babylon and Assyria) returned to Jerusalem and Canaan in an attempt to restore their religion. (The historical reporting of this return is by Ezra and Nehemiah.)

(g) The writing of Malachi, around 400 B.C., is the last date of Old Testament writing.

(h) Three world powers reigned during the years of the prophets: Assyrian, Neo-Babylonian, and Persian. Much of the prophets' message was about Gentile nations; some of it was even directed to them (e.g., Jonah).

2. Picture the land areas involved in the historical events noted above. This is shown on Map 1, Audience of the Prophets.

3. Observe on Chart A the sixteen names of prophets who were biblical authors. Note when they lived and what phase of

---

4. A rift had begun to form earlier than this date. Read 1 Sam. 11:8; 15:4; and 18:6, where a distinction is made between Israel and Judah.

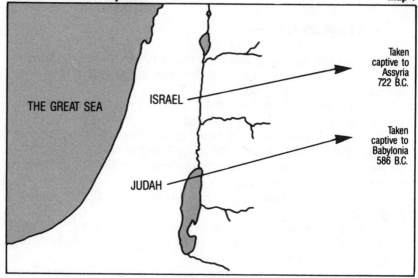

THE GREAT SEA

ISRAEL

JUDAH

Taken captive to Assyria 722 B.C.

Taken captive to Babylonia 586 B.C.

Jewish history their ministry was related to. Note, for example, that Jonah, Amos, and Hosea, in that chronological order, were prophets of Israel.[5] Actually, Jonah is different from the other two in that while he was a prophet within the commonwealth of Israel, his ministry described in the book was directed to a foreign nation, not to Israel. The prophets Jonah, Amos, and Hosea are the ones studied in this manual.

4. Chart B shows the three groups of minor prophets: (1) prophets of Israel, (2) prophets of Judah, and (3) post-exilic prophets. These are the groups studied in the three books of this self-study series on the minor prophets.

5. With the above historical setting in mind, think about the spiritual condition of God's people—the usual audience of the prophets. Wicked kings led multitudes of people into idolatry and all forms of disobedience to God. Periods of prosperity in the land of Canaan lured the people to a spirit of apathy and pleasure-seeking. Intermarriage with pagans broke down the institution of the home. Apostasy of the religious leaders meant neglect and eventual rejection of the Scriptures and true worship. People rebelled against God, but His long-suffering endured. Through the

5. Most of the dates of the prophets and rulers cited in this manual are those shown on John C. Whitcomb's study-graph, *Chart of Old Testament Kings and Prophets* (Chicago: Moody, 1968). The names of the sixteen prophets noted above appear on Chart B.

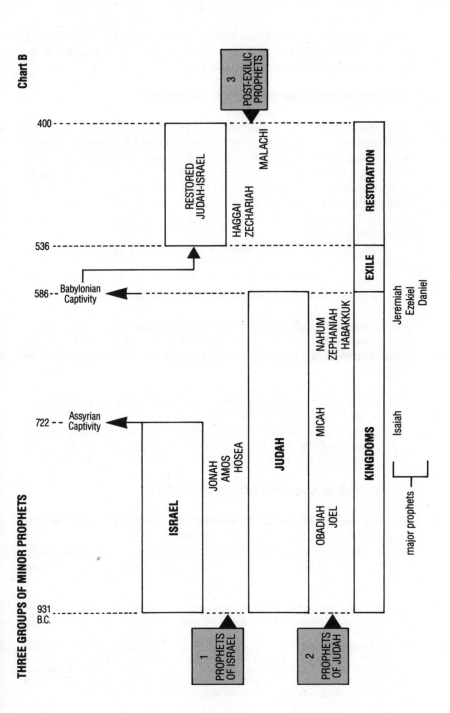

**Chart B**

**THREE GROUPS OF MINOR PROPHETS**

- **1** PROPHETS OF ISRAEL
- **2** PROPHETS OF JUDAH
- **3** POST-EXILIC PROPHETS

931 B.C.

ISRAEL

JUDAH

RESTORED JUDAH-ISRAEL

722 — Assyrian Captivity

586 — Babylonian Captivity

536

400

JONAH AMOS HOSEA

OBADIAH JOEL — MICAH — NAHUM ZEPHANIAH HABAKKUK

HAGGAI ZECHARIAH MALACHI

KINGDOMS — EXILE — RESTORATION

Isaiah — Jeremiah Ezekiel Daniel

major prophets

13

voice of the prophets, He sought to woo them to Himself. And the prophets were faithful to their calling. What they preached is recorded for us in the books of *The Twelve*.

## III. MAIN SUBJECTS OF THE MINOR PROPHETS

F. W. Farrar calls the writings of the Hebrew prophets—minor as well as major—"the crown and flower of the Old Testament writings."[6] It is unfortunate therefore that many Christians overlook studying Old Testament prophecy. The setting is ancient, to be sure: God's message to Israel and surrounding nations. But the applications of the principles are timeless and are therefore contemporary. Enhancing this is the imminency of fulfillment of end-times prophecies.

Let us look a little more at the content of the prophetic books.

### A. Instruction and Exhortation (forthtelling)

Many chapters deal with sin, warning, and judgment, but they do so because that is the very setting of God's good news of redemption. There is a positive, bright evangel in every book of *The Twelve*:

> The irrepressible love of God to sinful men; the perseverance and pursuits of His grace; His mercies that follow the exile and outcast; His truth that goes forth richly upon the heathen; the hope of the Saviour of mankind; the outpouring of the Spirit; counsels of patience; impulses of tenderness and of healing.[7]

### B. Prediction and Exhortation (foretelling)

The utterances of the prophets, for the most part, centered on four points in history: (1) their own times, (2) the threatening captivities (Assyrian and Babylonian) and eventual restoration, (3) the coming of their Messiah,[8] and (4) the reign of the Messiah as King.

---

6. F. W. Farrar, *The Minor Prophets* (New York: Randolph, n.d.), p. 21.
7. George Adam Smith, *The Book of The Twelve Prophets* (New York: Harper, n.d.), 1:9.
8. The name "Messiah" (lit., "anointed one") appears only twice in the Old Testament: Dan. 9:25-26. The idea of an anointed person or thing, however, is common in the Old Testament. In 2 Sam. 7 the concept of a Davidic Messiah originates, without using either the word "Messiah" or "anointed." In the prophets Christ is referred to by various names (e.g., "ruler," Mic. 5:2).

## 1. *The Four Prophetic Points*

Look at the diagram of Chart C. The prophet is standing on some high point (A), looking off into the distance (the future) and writing what he sees. Most often he sees the sins prevailing in his day among his own people (1 on the chart). Then he sees the impending crucial events (2), when the nation would be taken out of its land into captivity and later regathered. At times the Spirit enables him to look further into the future and to foretell the coming of the Messiah, the anointed One (Christ, 3). Occasionally he sees the most distant event, when the Messiah as the Son of David will establish a kingdom of peace and glory on this earth (4).

**FOUR PROPHETIC POINTS**        **Chart C**

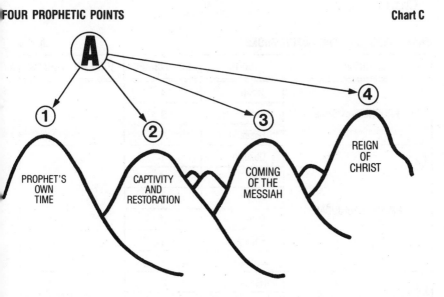

## 2. *The Two Messianic Themes*

When a prophet speaks of the coming Deliverer (Christ), he refers to Him in either of His two comings—either in the first coming as the suffering Messiah (e.g., Zech. 13:7) or in the second coming as the reigning Messiah (e.g., Zech. 14:9, 16). The prophets apparently were not aware that a long interval of time would transpire between Christ's manifestation in suffering (first advent, leading to the cross) and His revelation in glory (second advent, climaxing in the crown). Christ's suffering and His reigning appeared to them to be very close in time.[9]

In order to understand what future event a prophet is writing about, the Bible student must observe carefully the language and the content of the prophet's prediction.[10] This manual will give help in such studies as these.

## IV. JONAH, AMOS, AND HOSEA

The three books to be studied in this manual are Jonah, Amos, and Hosea.[11] The groupings of the twelve minor prophets as shown of Chart D explain why these three are studied together. (Note: Within each group the books are listed in chronological order. See Chart B.)

**THREE GROUPS OF THE TWELVE BOOKS**  Chart D

| GROUP | | BOOK | NO. of CHAPS. | TOTAL NO. of CHAPS. |
|---|---|---|---|---|
| (1) PROPHETS of ISRAEL | | Jonah | 4 | 27 |
| | | Amos | 9 | |
| | | Hosea | 14 | |
| (2) PROPHETS of JUDAH | | Obadiah | 1 | 20 |
| | | Joel | 3 | |
| | | Micah | 7 | |
| | | Nahum | 3 | |
| | | Habakkuk | 3 | |
| | | Zephaniah | 3 | |
| (3) POST-EXILIC PROPHETS | | Haggai | 2 | 20 |
| | | Zechariah | 14 | |
| | | Malachi | 4 | |

9. The prophets themselves knew that the Spirit had not revealed *all* details to them. Read 1 Pet. 1:10-11; Col. 1:26-27 (cf. Dan. 12:8-9).
10. Sometimes a prophecy may have a *multiple* intention of fulfillment. Here is an example: A prophecy of restoration of the Jews may concern (1) return from Babylonian captivity *and* (2) the regathering of Israel from all parts of the world in the end times.
11. The other two manuals on the minor prophets in this self-study series treat the second and third groups shown on Chart D.

Chart E shows which kings were reigning in Israel during the public ministries of each of the three prophets.[12] In a few instances there were co-regencies (e.g., both Jehoash and Jeroboam II ruled between 793 and 782). How many kings reigned during Hosea's ministry? Note that the Assyrians took Israel captive toward the close of Hosea's ministry. Since the captivity was God's judgment for sin, what does this reveal about the spiritual burden on Hosea's shoulders?

**KINGS CONTEMPORARY**                                       **Chart E**
**WITH THE MINOR PROPHETS OF ISRAEL**

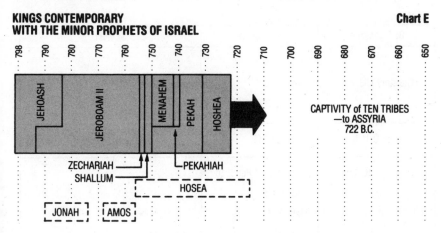

Below are listed the approximate dates of the reigns of Israel's kings and ministries of its prophets between 798 and 713 B.C.

| Reigns of the Kings | | Ministries of the Prophets | |
|---|---|---|---|
| Jehoash | 798-782 | | |
| Jeroboam II | 793-753 | Jonah | 784-722 |
| Zechariah | 753-752 | | |
| Shallum | 752 | Amos | 765-755 |
| Menahem | 752-742 | | |
| Pekahiah | 742-740 | Hosea | 755-713 |
| Pekah | 752-732 | | |
| Hoshea | 732-722 | | |

## V. NEW TESTAMENT QUOTES OF JONAH, AMOS, AND HOSEA

It is significant that the minor prophets are more frequently quoted than the major prophets in the New Testament. This con-

---

12. As noted earlier, Jonah's ministry was directed to a foreign power, Assyria. See "Chart of Kings and Prophets," in the self-study guide of 1 Kings, pp. 110-11, for a survey of all the kings and prophets of Israel and Judah.

firms the observation noted earlier that the word "minor" does not suggest that the minor prophets preached a less important message than the major prophets.

Below is a list of quotes or allusions to Jonah, Amos, and Hosea as found in the New Testament. Read each of the Old Testament passages and its quote, and record the subject in a few words. (Note: In the case of Jonah, no verse is quoted. Rather, the story itself is recognized by the New Testament text.)

| O. T. passage | N. T. quote | Subject |
|---|---|---|
| (The story of Jonah) | Matt. 16:4<br>Luke 11:30<br>Matt. 12:39-41 | |
| Amos 9:11-12 | Acts 15:16-17 | |
| Hosea 1:9-10; 2:23<br>10:8<br>11:1<br>6:2<br>13:14<br>6:6 | Rom. 9:25; 1 Pet. 2:10<br>Luke 23:30<br>Matt. 2:15<br>1 Cor. 15:4<br>1 Cor. 15:55<br>Matt. 9:13; 12:7 | |

**REVIEW QUESTIONS**

1. Name the twelve minor prophets in the order given in our English Bible.

2. Name the minor prophets according to the three groupings given in this lesson.

3. What does the title "minor prophets" signify?

4. What group name does the Hebrew Bible assign to these books?

5. What were some of the main ministries of prophets in Old Testament times? Distinguish between oral and writing prophets.

6. During what era of Jewish history did the writing prophets serve?

7. Who was the reigning world power during the ministries of Jonah, Amos, and Hosea?

8. Distinguish between forthtelling and foretelling, as far as the prophets were concerned. Which of these two was their writing mostly about?

9. What are the four prophetic points that appear in the prophets' messages?

10. What are the two different kinds of predictions concerning the coming of the Messiah?

\* \* \*

The three prophets of Israel have been compared this way:

Jonah:    prophet of a broken ministry
Amos:    prophet of the broken law
Hosea:   prophet of a broken heart

These comparisons suggest in a limited way something of the paths that your studies will follow as you move from book to book in this manual. Ask the Holy Spirit to be your Teacher, Guide, and Inspirer that you may grow stronger as a Christian by studying these words of God.

# Lesson 2
# Background and Survey of Jonah

**T**he story of Jonah is one of the clearest demonstrations of God's love and mercy for all mankind. This universal love is a foundational truth of the whole Bible, taught by the most-quoted verse, John 3:16. By studying Jonah before the other prophets we will see the full view first—God's love for Gentile *and* Jew—and this will put our later studies about Israel and Judah in proper perspective.

## I. BACKGROUND

Before making a survey of the book itself, there are some interesting things to be learned about the man Jonah and the book bearing his name.

### A. The Man Jonah

1. *Name and family*
The name Jonah (Heb., *Yonah*) means "dove." According to 2 Kings 14:25, he was the son of Amittai[1] and his hometown was Gath-hepher. This village was located about three miles northeast of Nazareth, Jesus' hometown.[2] Recall that the great prophet Jeremiah was also from a small, little-known town, Anathoth (Jer. 1:1). What does this teach you about God's ways in the choices of His servants?
2. *Ministry as a prophet*
Jonah probably had the same general qualifications for the office of prophet as did the other prophets. Most of his character

---

1. There is a Jewish tradition that Jonah's mother was the widow who fed Elijah at Zarephath (1 Kings 17:8-24).
2. Read the Pharisees' statement of John 7:52 about prophets coming out of Galilee. Were the Pharisees correct?

traits revealed in the narrative of his book are not commendable (e.g., disobedience and pouting), but this underscores God's patience and willingness to work through men despite their frailties. Jonah must have been an honest man to write such a dark picture of himself. And we must not overlook how Jesus associated Jonah with Solomon when referring to the great impact of their ministries (Matt. 12:41-42).

The main purpose of the book of Jonah is to show God's gracious dealings with the pagan Gentile city of Nineveh. God chose Jonah to be His channel of communication to its residents.

Chart F shows Jonah and some of his contemporaries. Note the following:

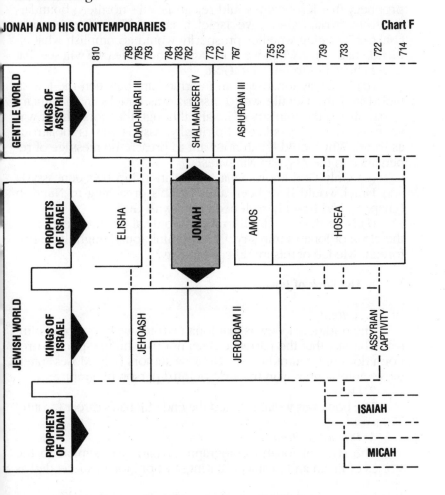

**JONAH AND HIS CONTEMPORARIES**          **Chart F**

(a) Elisha was Jonah's predecessor. In fact Jonah may have been one of Elisha's disciples, learning much from this "man of God." Read 2 Kings 13:14-20 for the account of Elisha's death. Amos and Hosea were Jonah's successors.

(b) Even though the book of Jonah is about the prophet's ministry to the foreign city of Nineveh, Jonah was primarily a prophet of Israel to Israel. However, God did not choose to record in Scripture any details of his homeland ministry beyond what we learn from a passage in 2 Kings (see below).

(c) Jeroboam II, the most powerful king of Israel, reigned during all of Jonah's public ministry. Read 2 Kings 14:23-29 for a summary of Jeroboam's evil reign. Note the reference to Jonah's prophecy that Jeroboam would regain Israel's northern boundaries from Syria. "God gave Israel a last chance of repentance [14:26-27], seeing whether prosperity would accomplish what affliction had not."[3] When we study Amos and Hosea we will see that Israel chose not to return to God.

(d) In a way Jonah was an intermediary between the Jewish world and the Gentile world. Assyria was Israel's main military threat during the ministry of Jonah, although the worst threat was yet to come (50 years later). Spiritually, Assyria was as idolatrous as Israel. Why would Jonah not want to preach the message of repentance to the Assyrian Ninevites?

(e) Only God knows what the relationship between Assyria and Israel would have been after Jonah's preaching to Nineveh (chap. 3), had Israel herself been right with God.

(f) Note that Israel fell to Assyria only about fifty years after the close of Jonah's ministry. Do you think Jonah might have had foreknowledge of this imminent captivity?

### B. The Book of Jonah

1. *Author*
The traditional view is that Jonah wrote this book about himself. The fact that the narrative does not use the first-person pronoun does not contradict this. Hebrew authors (e.g., Moses) often wrote autobiography in the style of third-person biography.

2. *Date*
The book was written toward the end of Jonah's career (around 770 B.C.).

3. *Type of writing*
The style of Jonah is biographical narrative, similar to the stories of Elijah and Elisha (1, 2 Kings) whom Jonah succeeded as

3. H. L. Ellison, "I and II Kings," in *The New Bible Commentary*, p. 325.

prophet.[4] Hidden in the historical account is a predictive, typical purpose. Here are two types:

(a) *Jonah and the whale.* It prefigured Christ's burial and resurrection. Read Matthew 12:39-41. In Old Testament times God's people would not have seen this hidden prophecy or type (unless the Holy Spirit would disclose such an interpretation to them in a particular situation).

(b) *Jonah's mission to Nineveh.* This prefigured the history of Israel in many striking ways, as described by Henrietta Mears:

> Jonah was called to a world mission. So was Israel. [Gen. 12:3b]
> Jonah refused to fulfill his God-appointed mission. So did Israel.
> Jonah was punished by being cast into the sea. Israel was scattered among the nations.
> Jonah was preserved. So has Israel's identity been preserved.
> Jonah repented and was cast out of the fish and restored to life. Israel shall be cast out by all the nations and restored to her former position.
> Jonah, obedient to God, goes on his mission. Israel in obedience shall become a witness to all the earth.
> Jonah was blessed in that Nineveh was brought to salvation. Israel shall be blessed in the conversion extending to the whole world.[5]

Do you think believers in Israel living in Jonah's day might have looked upon Jonah's experience as symbolizing these events to come for Israel? Jonah's deliverance from the belly of the whale was also a sign to the Ninevites. What did it signify, according to Jesus? (Read Luke 11:29-30.)

4. *Purposes*

Three main purposes of the book of Jonah are—

(a) to teach God's people their responsibility to deliver the message of salvation to all people—Jew and Gentile;[6]

(b) to demonstrate that God honors repentance for sin, whoever the person (cf. Jer. 18:7-10; read Rom. 1:16; 2:9-10; 3:29; 2 Pet. 3:9; Mark 16:15);

---

4. In the Hebrew Bible, 1 and 2 Kings are classified among the Former Prophets, and Jonah among the Latter Prophets.
5. Henrietta C. Mears, *What the Bible Is All About* (Glendale: Gospel Light, 1953), p. 303. This is sometimes called the allegorical interpretation of the book of Jonah.
6. Acts 10-11 and Romans 9-11 show the application to this in New Testament times when the early Jewish Christians hesitated to accept Gentile believers into their fellowship.

(c) to show to people of the Christian era that Christ's death and resurrection, prefigured in Jonah's experience, were in the divine plan before Christ ever walked this earth.

5. *The geography of Jonah*

Map 2, Geography of Jonah, shows the three key geographical points in the story of Jonah: Jonah's homeland, Tarshish, and Nineveh.

**GEOGRAPHY OF JONAH**                                        **Map 2**

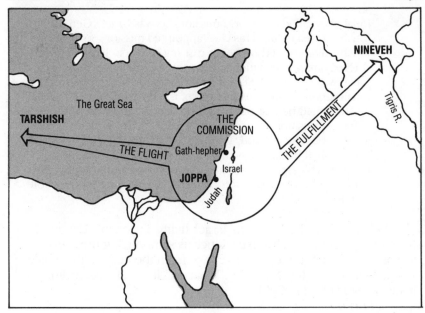

(a) The homeland—the place where God commissioned Jonah to go to Nineveh. This was Israel, north of Judah. Exactly where Jonah was when the call of 1:2 came is not known. Shown on the map are Gath-hepher, Jonah's hometown, and Joppa, where he boarded a ship to go to Tarshish.

(b) Tarshish—the city where Jonah wanted to flee to hide from the presence of the Lord. It may have been the city of Tartessus of southwestern Spain.

(c) Nineveh—the earliest reference to Nineveh in the Bible is in Genesis 10:11-12. Read these verses and observe the references to Rehoboth, Calah, and Resen. It appears that these three adjoining cities were part of the Nineveh city-state district, and that the whole area, by virtue of its size, was referred to as a "great city."

Nineveh was 500 miles northeast of the Sea of Galilee, located on the banks of the Tigris River.

6. *The amazing whale story*

Jonah's experience with the whale ("great fish," 1:17) obviously was of miraculous proportions. On various occasions men since Jonah's day have survived the ordeal of being swallowed by a whale.[7] Actually many miracles were involved in Jonah's experience, as we shall see in the next lesson. Frank Gaebelein says, "The miracle consisted in God's divine appointment and control of the sea monster (whatever it might have been) in making it play its creaturely part in His dealing with His disobedient prophet."[8]

All miracles are beyond human comprehension. Only faith in the Miracle-Worker, God, can satisfy the natural question, "How?" This is why the whale story is credible to the Christian, though incredible to the skeptic.

## II. SURVEY

The book of Jonah is one of the easiest and most interesting books to read in the Bible. One author says it is the most beautiful story ever written in so small a compass. Our approach to the book is to survey its structure, to see its large, overall thrust. Then we will be prepared to analyze the individual chapters. The order of study is stated by the familiar rule "Image the whole, then execute the parts."

### A. A Survey Reading

1. Scan the four chapters for overall impressions. Does the book have a natural opening? What about a conclusion?

2. Is there progression in the plot? Who is the main person in the action? Are any other individuals involved?

### B. A Survey Chart

Chart G is a survey of the account of Jonah. Observe the following in connection with the chart:

1. The book is of two main parts. What three outlines on the chart show this?

2. Study carefully the bottom of the chart that compares the narratives of the two halves of the book. Note similarities and dif-

---

7. See Gleason L. Archer, *A Survey of Old Testament Introduction*, p. 302 fn., for a description of one of these deliverances.
8. Frank Gaebelein, *Four Minor Prophets*, p. 131.

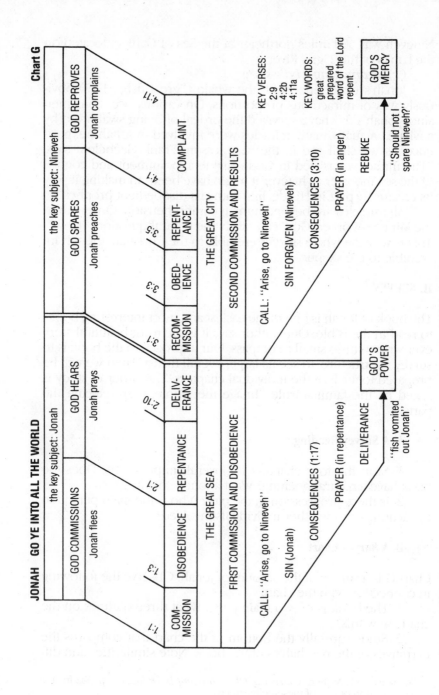

# JONAH GO YE INTO ALL THE WORLD

Chart G

| | the key subject: Jonah | | | the key subject: Nineveh | | | |
|---|---|---|---|---|---|---|---|
| GOD COMMISSIONS | | GOD HEARS | | GOD SPARES | | | GOD REPROVES |
| Jonah flees | | Jonah prays | | Jonah preaches | | | Jonah complains |
| COM-MISSION | DISOBEDIENCE | REPENTANCE | DELIV-ERANCE | RECOM-MISSION | OBED-IENCE | REPENT-ANCE | COMPLAINT |
| 1:1 | 1:3 | 2:1 | 2:10 | 3:1 | 3:3 | 3:5 | 4:1 | 4:11 |

THE GREAT SEA
THE GREAT CITY

FIRST COMMISSION AND DISOBEDIENCE
SECOND COMMISSION AND RESULTS

CALL: "Arise, go to Nineveh"
CALL: "Arise, go to Nineveh"

SIN (Jonah)
SIN FORGIVEN (Nineveh)

CONSEQUENCES (1:17)
CONSEQUENCES (3:10)

PRAYER (in repentance)
PRAYER (in anger)

DELIVERANCE
REBUKE

KEY VERSES:
2:9
4:2b
4:11a

KEY WORDS:
great
prepared
word of the Lord
repent

**GOD'S POWER** — "fish vomited out Jonah"

**GOD'S MERCY** — "Should not I spare Nineveh?"

26

ferences. Refer to the Bible text to support parts of the outlines that are not clear.

3. At some time during your study you may want to make your own outlines of the book. Record these in the blank oblique spaces.

4. Read the key verses shown. Note also the key words. Add to this list as you proceed with your study in the next two lessons.

* * *

## REVIEW QUESTIONS

1. What does the Hebrew name *Jonah* mean literally?

2. Where was Jonah's hometown located?

3. Did Jonah ever prophesy about his own land of Israel? If so, what book of the Bible reports this?

4. Who was king of Israel during all of Jonah's public ministry?

5. What prophet did Jonah succeed? What prophets succeeded him?

6. Who wrote the book of Jonah?

7. What part of Jonah's experience did Jesus interpret as prefiguring His own ministry?

8. What is the main teaching of this part of Scripture? What other important truths are taught?

9. Locate Tarshish and Nineveh with respect to Joppa.

10. Try to visualize the highlights of the survey chart. What are the two main parts of the book of Jonah? How does each part begin?

11. Does the book end on a high or low note as far as Jonah is concerned?

# Jonah Runs from God

The story of Jonah has much to say to a Christian fleeing from the Lord's call to service. And what believer has never been tempted to shirk his duty and so hide from the presence of the Lord? The truths about God and man that appear in these two chapters are basic and vital. Study the chapters not as mere history but as "history with purpose," even as the apostle Paul applied Israel's experiences: "Now all these things happened unto them for ensamples: and they are written for our admonition, upon whom the ends of the world are come" (1 Cor. 10:11).

## I. PREPARATION FOR STUDY

1. You will appreciate more what was going through Jonah's mind at the time of his first commissioning (1:2) if you understand why he was such a zealous patriot for the cause of Israel. As a prophet of God he surely knew and preached about the ever-present spiritual wickedness of Israel that threatened their very survival. But as a patriot, Jonah believed that the political threat of Assyria against Israel was always to be reckoned with. A couple of times destruction had almost come; the prophet was convinced that sooner or later it would surely fall. And then (Jonah must have thought) would the Assyrian conqueror be a tyrant like one of his predecessors, Ashur-nasirpal II (883-859)? Jonah shuddered when he thought of the infamous reputation of that king:

> His usual procedure after the capture of a hostile city was to burn it, and then to mutilate all the grown male prisoners by cutting off their hands and ears and putting out their eyes; after which they were piled up in a great heap to perish in torture from sun, flies, their wounds and suffocation; the children, both

boys and girls, were all burnt alive at the stake; and the chief was carried off to Assyria to be flayed alive for the king's delectation.[1]

Even in Jonah's time the Ninevites were known as a violent people (3:8b). So when Jonah heard that God wanted him to preach to Nineveh, capital of Assyria, probably his only thought was, *"Suppose the people repent—will God then spare them? And if they are spared, will they eventually conquer us?"* In the words of Ellison:

> Men were hoping and praying that the scourge might be vanquished, but here was God holding out His hand of mercy to the threatened city. Jonah must have known that this could mean only one thing, that God was preparing Assyria to finish the work of judgment foretold to Elijah at Horeb some seventy years earlier.[2]

2. Read Jonah 4:1-2 in *The Living Bible*, if this paraphrase is available to you. Did Jonah have a correct knowledge of the sovereignty and power of God?

3. Only one of the twenty-seven verses of these two chapters is specifically about Nineveh (1:2). Do not let this disproportion keep you from continually relating Jonah's experiences to the very reason of his commission: *the lost estate of Gentile Nineveh.*

## II. ANALYSIS

*Segments to be analyzed*: 1:1-17 and 2:1-10
*Paragraph divisions*: at verses 1:1, 4, 11, 17; 2:1, 4, 7, 10. (Mark these in your Bible.)

### A. General Analysis of Chapter 1

Chart H is a work sheet for recording your observations of the highlights of the first chapter. Record in the boxes what is done and said by each of these: God, Jonah, the sailors.

---

1. H. R. Hall, *The Ancient History of the Near East*, p. 445, quoted by H. L. Ellison in *The Prophets of Israel*, p. 57.
2. Ellison, p. 60.

| | Jonah and God | | Jonah and the Sailors | | Jonah and God |
|---|---|---|---|---|---|
| | **FLIGHT** | | **PANIC** | **SUPPLICATION** | **"BURIAL"** |
| | 1:1 | 1:4 | 1:11 | 1:17 | |
| **GOD** | | | | | |
| **JONAH** | | | | | |
| **SAILORS** | | | | | |

### B. Paragraph Analysis

1. *Paragraph 1:1-3*
What two different phrases with the word "Lord" appear here? Relate a prophet's ministry to each one.

_____

_____

What was to be the theme of Jonah's preaching?

_____

Read 1:1-2 again. Why did Jonah refuse this commission to preach?

_____

_____

2. *Paragraph 1:4-10*
What different miracles are recorded in these verses?

_____

_____

What was the religion of the mariners (1:5)?

_____

Compare "his god" (1:5) with "thy God" (1:6). In both verses the Hebrew word is the same: *Elohim* (of Gen. 1). How much did Jonah tell the sailors concerning his beliefs? Observe that he identified *his* god as "the Lord" (Heb., *Jehovah*). Why would he tell them that he was fleeing from the presence of the Lord (1:10)?

_____

_____

3. *Paragraph 1:11-16*
Can you think of a reason that the sailors delayed throwing Jonah into the sea (1:13)?

_____

_____

How many times does the title "Lord" (*Jehovah*) appear in this paragraph?

_____

Can you explain why the sailors addressed God by this name, whereas earlier the shipmaster had referred to him only as God (*Elohim*, 1:6)?

_____

_____

What kind of belief, if any, did the sailors have, as of verse 14?

_____

Do you think their fear and acts of devotion, as reported by verse 16, came from contrite sinners who were forsaking their idols and turning to the Lord for their soul's salvation?

_____

Do you think their offerings were made merely to appease God's wrath? (Cf. 2:9.)

_____

31

4. *Paragraph 1:17*

What do you think is meant by the word "prepared"? (See *Notes*.)

---

Compare the three *greats* in chapter 1: "great city" (1:2); "great wind" (1:4); "great fish" (1:17³).

---

---

---

Can you visualize what was going through Jonah's mind during his conscious hours as he lay in the belly of the fish for three days?

---

---

Had Jonah prayed to God while he was on the ship?

---

Had the sailors prayed?

---

### C. General Analysis of Chapter 2

God has recorded in His Scriptures this touching prayer of repentance as an example of the contrite heart that He honors and blesses. Spend much time here. Extend your studies beyond the suggestions given.

1. Note that Jonah's prayer is the only thing recorded between his being swallowed up (1:17) and his being vomited out (2:10). What does this emphasize?

2. Chart I is a work sheet for recording your observations. The prayer is divided into three parts. See if you can arrive at some outlines showing patterns in the prayer.⁴ Use the blank spaces inside the large boxes for recording key words and phrases of the Bible text. Use the narrow boxes and margins for recording your outlines and other observations.

3. Is this a prayer for deliverance from the great fish or praise for deliverance from death?

---

3. In the Hebrew Bible this verse is placed at the beginning of chap. 2.
4. Much can be learned by analyzing prayers in the Bible. For example, the petitions of the "Lord's Prayer" of Matt. 6:9-13 follow this general pattern: the first three concern God and His program; the last four, man and his needs.

2:1

I called ... he answered

Jonah calling
out, for
God to save
him. God listens

4 God saving

- Jonah feeling
repentant

7 Jonah is thankful
- God is the only
one who can save!

9

33

4. What did Jonah say about the following:
(a) his own heart

distress, remembering?,

(b) the Lord

(c) his intentions

5. Compare 2:10 with 2:1.

Also compare 2:10 with 1:1.

## III. NOTES

1. *"Nineveh, that great city"* (1:2). Nineveh was a complex of cities, the largest of the world in Jonah's day. For defense, the inner city was surrounded by a thick wall 100 feet high. Population of the district has been estimated as many as 600,000.

2. *"Their wickedness"* (1:2). Gross idolatry, immorality, and cult worship were among Nineveh's glaring sins. Read Nahum 3 for a prophet's description of judgment for Nineveh's idolatry.

3. *"Prepared a great fish"* (1:17). This may have been a whale, but not necessarily.[5] Some think it was a certain species of shark. Whatever it was, it was specially prepared (chosen, appointed, and directed) to swallow Jonah. (Cf. 4:6-8, where God is said to have "prepared" a gourd, a worm, and an east wind. The same Hebrew word for "prepare" appears at one other place in the Bible, Ps. 61:7. Most versions translate it by "appoint.")

4. *"Three days and three nights"* (1:17). This was not necessarily seventy-two hours, even as Jesus was not necessarily in the grave for that many hours. The phrase implies three consecutive solar days, but the first and last can be shorter than a day.

5. *"Belly of hell"* (2:2). The translation "hell" is misleading. The Hebrew word is *Sheol*, which was where the spirits of de-

5. The Greek word *ketos* translated "whale" in Matt. 12:40, is better translated "sea monster" (NASB and *Berkeley*). The phrase "great fish" in John 1:17 is very adequate.

34

ceased persons went at death to await their eternal disposition. Jonah likened the inside of the fish to a kind of grave.

6. *"Lying vanities"* (2:8). The whole verse might be paraphrased thus: "They that worship false gods cut themselves off from the God of mercy." Do you think Jonah might have meant by this that the Ninevites deserved judgment because they rejected God? Read Psalm 31:6, which has the same phrase.

## IV. FOR THOUGHT AND DISCUSSION

1. Read John 15:16. What is involved in being chosen by God for a particular task? What was Jonah's sin of presumption?

2. Read Romans 3:29. With the lessons of Jonah in mind, how would you apply apply this verse to today?

3. How does a Christian flee from "the presence of the Lord"? Can anyone *really* escape God? Read Psalm 139.

4. Jonah was willing to save the sailors' lives, but he did not want God to leave a door open for Nineveh's deliverance. What are your reactions?

5. We are not told how the sailors fared in the months that followed this experience. If their response of 1:16 was in proportion to the spiritual light given them, do you think God gave them further light so that they might come to know Him personally?

6. God spared Jonah despite his defection. Is this the way of God's will in the lives of all His children at all times? (Cf. Ps. 106:13-15.)

7. Why do you think God used such a dramatic method of saving Jonah from drowning as that of being swallowed by a great fish? In answering, apply Luke 11:30a. Do you think news about Jonah's deliverance reached Nineveh before he finally arrived there? If so, may the sailors have been the ones to spread the word?

8. What have you learned from this lesson about repentance and prayer?

## V. FURTHER STUDY

1. Study Jesus' applications of Jonah's "whale" experience as a sign of His death and burial (Matt. 12:40). Note that He did not tell the Pharisees *how* He would arrive in "the heart of the earth." At a later time He told His disciples that He would "be killed, and be raised again the third day" (Matt. 16:21).

2. When God's children have been confined to prison for a length of time, one of their best sources of strength has been

Scripture, including the Psalms.[6] Jonah did not have a biblical scroll in his hand when he was swallowed by the fish, but he remembered some of his favorite psalms. The prayer of chapter 2 does not quote verses from Psalms, but some of its lines are reminiscent of that book. Compare the lists shown below by reading the Bible texts.

| Psalms | Jonah |
|---|---|
| 88:3-4; 103:4a | 2:2b |
| 18:6; 31:22 | 2:2 |
| 42:7b | 2:3 |
| 69:1-2 | 2:5 |
| 30:3 | 2:6b |
| 5:7; 142:4-5 | 2:7 |
| 50:14, 23 | 2:9 |
| 3:8 | 2:9b |

## VI. WORDS TO PONDER

Jonah prayed to the Lord *from inside the fish*:

I will never worship anyone but you! For how can I thank you enough for all you have done? (Jonah 2:9, *The Living Bible*).

6. Paul and Silas in the jail at Philippi (Acts 16:25) and John Bunyan are two good examples.

# Jonah Preaches to Nineveh

When a man fails, he does not always get a second chance; Jonah got one, by God's grace. The words of the text reporting this are simple yet crucial: "And the word of the Lord came unto Jonah the second time" (3:1). God miraculously spared Jonah from death and recommissioned him, but not only for the restoration and blessing of the prophet. God still had in His heart the tens of thousands of idolatrous Ninevites who needed to hear the message of redemption. He could have sent another prophet to them, but He chose to let Jonah's deliverance be a sign to the Ninevites, attesting that his message was from God (Luke 11:30).

Jesus said that Jonah's mission was successful, for Nineveh "repented at the preaching of Jonah" (Luke 11:32). However, the sequel to that mission in the life of the prophet was grievous. These are the two subjects that we shall be studying in this lesson.

## I. PREPARATION FOR STUDY

1. Keep in mind the main subject of the book of Jonah, which is God's preaching to Gentile Nineveh through a Jewish prophet. It is true that most of Old Testament history is about the Jews as God's people, whom He chose "most of all in order that they might be prepared as the nation in which, when God's time was ready, the Saviour of the world might be born."[1] But God did not want Israel to keep to themselves what He had revealed to them. He wanted them to share His truth with the nations of the world so that all might come to know Him. They should not despise

---

1. F. F. Bruce, *The Books and the Parchments* (Westwood, N.J.: Revell, 1963), p. 78.

Gentile nations but consider them as objects of God's love also.[2] God's commission to Jews to be "missionaries" to Gentiles appears at various places in the Old Testament. Read Isaiah 49:6 for an example. Note how clearly the mission is spelled out:

> I will also give thee for a light to the Gentiles, that thou mayest be my salvation unto the end of the earth.

2. Review the survey Chart G, with its title in mind. Chart J shows excerpts from the survey chart.

**THE CONTEXT OF 3:1—4:11**                                                            **Chart J**

| 1:1 | 2:1 | 3:1 | 4:1 | 4:11 |
|---|---|---|---|---|
| the key subject: Jonah | | the key subject: Nineveh | | |
| FIRST COMMISSION and DISOBEDIENCE | | SECOND COMMISSION and RESULTS | | |
| | | JONAH PREACHES | JONAH COMPLAINS | |

Note especially that the key subject of chapters 3-4 is Nineveh. Jonah is prominent throughout these chapters, but all his talking is either to or about the Ninevites.

## II. ANALYSIS

*Segments to be analyzed*: 3:1-10 and 4:1-11
*Paragraph divisions*: at verses 3:1, 5, 10; 4:1, 5, 9 (Mark these in your Bible.)

### A. General Analysis

1. Scan the two chapters for overall impressions.

2. One example of how the Jews' bigotry and contempt carried over into the early centuries A.D. is the Jewish Talmud's reference to Gentiles as "the spittle that falleth from a man's mouth." See Ralph Earle, *Meet the Minor Prophets* (Kansas City: Beacon Hill, n.d.), p. 55.

2. Refer again to the extended outline shown at the bottom of survey Chart G. Identify each line of the outline with the particular paragraph of chapters 3-4, which it represents.

3. Who does most of the speaking in chapter 3? Who are the speakers of chapter 4? Compare the tone (atmosphere) of chapter 3 with that of chapter 4. Underline in your Bible a word from 4:11 and one from 3:4 that are in contrast to each other.

4. Compare 4:11 with 2:10, as to attributes of God. (See Chart G.)

### B. Paragraph Analysis

1. *Nineveh Repents*: Chapter 3
(a) *Paragraph 3:1-4*
What are three key facts of this paragraph?

_40 more days!_

_Word came to Jonah for a second time_

_Jonah obeyed_

What was Jonah's message?

_Nineveh will be destroyed_

Does it sound as though his prophecy was unconditional—that doom was inevitable, regardless?[3]

Anyone could have stood before the Ninevites and proclaimed the doom of 3:4. Probably many had even done it. But what made Jonah's preaching unique?

Do you think Jonah knew that if Nineveh repented, God would spare the city? (Recall why Jonah didn't want to preach to Nineveh in the first place.)

3. Sermons that are recorded in the Bible usually are condensed versions of what was originally delivered. There is no way to know how much more was spoken in the original situation. However, we may be confident that God inspired the reporting of all that would fulfill the purposes of the account.

(b) *Paragraph 3:5-9*
Write a list of the different things that the Ninevites did in responding to Jonah's preaching.

_fasted, sackcloth, sat in dust_

What is first on your list (3:5*a*)? How many of the populace were involved?

What is the first phrase of 3:5? Would the people have believed God if they had disbelieved Jonah's message?

What attended Jonah's message that made it trustworthy to them?

Read Genesis 37:34 for the Bible's first reference to sackcloth. Then see *Notes* concerning this mourning apparel. Why do you think the king included animals in his decree (3:7-8)? (Consider what animals would do if not fed.)

Note the two key words "cry" and "turn" in verse 8. What two things were the people to turn from?

_Evil ways violence_

How much hope of being spared did the king have (3:9)?

_Still had it_

Do you think Jonah preached about a possibility of sparing? (Cf. 3:4.)

(c) *Paragraph 3:10*
Complete the threesome:

God saw; God _had compassion_; God _did not destroy (forgave)_.
Did God see only the outward rituals of mourning? ("God saw their works.")

40

## 2. *Jonah Remonstrates*: Chapter 4

(a) *Paragraph 4:1-4*

What was Jonah's reaction to God's withholding judgment?

_Ticked off_

In verse 2 Jonah reminds God why he did not want to go to Nineveh in the first place. He acknowledges God's attribute of love. At least what does this reveal about Jonah?

_Not mindful of grace_

Can you understand why Jonah despaired of life at this point (4:3)?

_All for nothing_

(b) *Paragraph 4:5-8*

Does verse 5 suggest that maybe Jonah thought that *some* kind of judgment would fall upon Nineveh?

Do you think he counted the forty days carefully? _Yes_

This is a paragraph of parables in action. What three things did God miraculously prepare?

_Vine, worm, blazing sun_

What was the purpose of each, and what were Jonah's reactions?

(c) *Paragraph 4:9-11*

This the concluding paragraph of the book. It reads as an anticlimax as far as the drama about Jonah is concerned. But when God is seen as the key Person of the book, then the climax that had been reached at 3:10 is amplified by these last verses. Who has the last word?

Does it surprise you that no reply from Jonah is recorded?

41

How does God interpret and apply the parable of the gourd?

---

A key phrase of the book, shown on the survey Chart G, is 4:11*a*: "Should not I spare Nineveh?" The Hebrew word translated "spare" is better translated "pity." (The same Hebrew word is translated "pity" in v. 10.) What is your answer to this important question? "Should I not have compassion on Nineveh?" (v. 11, NASB). (Cf. Rom. 9:14-15.)

---

## III. NOTES

1. *"City of three days' journey"* (3:3). The "city" was probably the district including Nineveh, Rehoboth, Calah, and Resen, as noted earlier. The entire circuit of that area was more than sixty miles.[4] It is difficult to say whether the phrase "three days' journey" intends to measure a journey *around* the city or to tell how long Jonah took on his preaching mission *through* the city, stopping at various places along the way.[5] The phrase of 3:4*a* favors the latter interpretation.

2. *"Sackcloth"* (3:5). This was a coarse, dark cloth made of goat's hair, sometimes worn over an inner garment, sometimes over the bare skin. It symbolized grief, humility, and utter dependence on God.

3. *"King of Nineveh"* (3:6). Some think this was the ruler of the district of Nineveh. Others interpret the phrase as referring to the King of Assyria. The decree (3:7) applied only to Nineveh.

4. *"Sixscore thousand persons"* (4:11). The number 120,000 counts those who could not "discern between their right hand and their left hand." Various interpretations of this phrase include:

(a) Children who had not reached the age of choice between good and evil (*Berkeley* fn.)

(b) People outside of Israel who were ignorant of the law of God (*New Bible Commentary*)

---

4. See D. Robinson, "Jonah," in *The New Bible Commentary*, p. 718, for a discussion of size. Some say the diameter of the entire district may have been as long as sixty miles.
5. See Gleason Archer, *A Survey of Old Testament Introduction*, pp. 298-99.

(c) Infants and children who literally did not "know" their right hands from their left (TLB fn.)

(d) People in utter spiritual darkness (TLB).

## IV. FOR THOUGHT AND DISCUSSION

1. What spiritual truth is suggested by the combination "Arise, go" (3:2)?

2. What different attitudes of heart do you think are involved in genuine repentance? Note for example the two words "cry" and "turn" in 3:8.

3. What does the phrase "God repented" (3:10) mean in light of the unchanging character of God?

4. What is the difference, if any, between mercy and grace? (Cf. 4:2.) Refer to an exhaustive concordance and observe how often these words appear in the Old Testament.[6] Read Psalm 103:8-18 for a refreshing description of God's mercy.

5. Did an entire city ever turn to God as a result of Jesus' preaching? Does this mean that Jesus was less qualified to preach than Jonah? (Cf. Luke 11:32.)

6. Did Jonah know his own shortcoming (4:2)? How can a Christian be restored who has run away from a commission of God?

7. Do you think Israel should have learned an important spiritual lesson from Nineveh's repentance? If Israel had learned, there would not have been the captivity of 722 B.C. (See Chart F.)

## V. FURTHER STUDY

1. You may want to make an extended study of fasting in the Bible. A Bible dictionary will be of help in this.

2. Think more about the difference between God's grace and God's mercy. Grace deals with guilt of sin; mercy is for misery that is the consequence of that sin:

GRACE for GUILT
MERCY for MISERY

Richard Trench applies these two words to familiar New Testament verses:

---

6. Two recommended concordances are James Strong, *The Exhaustive Concordance of the Bible*, and Robert Young, *Analytical Concordance to the Bible.*

God so loved the world with a pitying love [mercy] that He gave his only begotten Son [grace], that the world through Him might be saved (cf. Ephes. ii.4; Luke i.78, 79).

But the two divine attributes manifest themselves in the experience of a sinner in this order: grace first, as the basis of mercy:

The righteousness of God . . . demands that the guilt should be done away, before the misery can be assuaged; only the forgiven may be blessed. He must pardon, before He can heal; men must be justified before they can be sanctified.[8]

Does this account for the order "grace, mercy" rather than "mercy, grace" in the apostolic benedictions (e.g., 1 Tim. 1:2; 2 Tim. 1:2; Titus 1:4)?

## VI. CONCLUSION

These are G. Campbell Morgan's concluding comments on the book of Jonah:

Thus the last picture we have of Jonah is that of a man still out of harmony with the tender mercy of God, and the last vision of Jehovah is that of a God full of pity and compassion even for a city such as Nineveh. . . . [The book reveals] a side of the Divine nature of which the people had no appreciation. It was a revelation far in advance of the age in which Jonah exercised his ministry. As a matter of fact, the people as a whole never came to understand it, and thus in his persistent displeasure Jonah represented the nation in its ultimate failure to understand the deepest truth concerning their God.[9]

7. Richard Trench, *Synonyms of the New Testament* (Grand Rapids: Eerdmans, 1948), p. 171.
8. Ibid.
9. G. Campbell Morgan, *The Analyzed Bible* (Westwood, N.J.: Revell, 1964), pp. 304-5.

# Lesson 5
# Background and Survey of Amos

**A**mos was God's prophet to prosperous Israel, steeped in religiosity, immorality, and complacency. Those evils plague our own land in this twentieth century, so it is not difficult to see how contemporary the book is. May God give us eyes to see and hearts to respond as we study this important Scripture.

"Behind the book there beats a life." So before we survey the contents of the book itself, let us learn about Amos the man, to feel the heartbeat of the prophet of Tekoa who bore a burden for Israel.

## I. BACKGROUND

### A. The Man Amos

1. *Name and family*
The name Amos means "burden-bearer" (from the Hebrew root *amas*, "to carry"). No reference is made in the book to any relative, including his father. The fact that his father is not named may suggest a humble birth. There is no reference to Amos in any other Bible book.[1]

Amos was a native of Tekoa, a small village six miles south of Bethlehem, overlooking the Dead Sea. The town was just a few miles from the busy caravan route linking Jerusalem with Hebron and Beersheba. (See map.) In this barren hill country, Amos was a herdsman of sheep and goats and a grower of sycamore figs (1:1; 7:14).[2] As a wool merchant he probably made many trips into the

---

1. The Amos of Luke 3:25 and Amoz of 2 Kings 20:1 are different persons.
2. Pastoral scenes abound in his book at these and other places: 1:2; 2:13; 3:4-5; 4:7; 6:12; 7:1; 8:1; 9:6. When God inspired men to write the Scriptures, He did not set aside such things as their personality and home background.

northern cities of Israel and saw firsthand the religious and social corruption of its people.

It is significant that Amos's home was in Judah, the Southern Kingdom, but God called him to preach mainly to Israel, the Northern Kingdom. Unlike Jonah, he was not so proud a patriot that he would not minister to "another people." Truly his name "burden-bearer" matched the man.

Amos was one of the most colorful personalities among the prophets. He was humble and rugged, a son of the wilderness, like Elijah and John the Baptist. He was fearless—he "feared God so much that he feared no one else at all."[3] And he was faithful to God in obeying the divine call to preach His Word. One writer says that his was "one of the most wonderful appearances in the history of the human spirit."[4]

### 2. Ministry as a prophet

God called Amos to be a prophet while he was tending his flock (7:15). Recall that David's commission came as he tended his sheep (1 Sam. 16:11-13); and Gideon was called from a threshing floor (Judg. 6:11-14). As noted above, Amos's ministry was mainly to the Northern Kingdom of Israel (1:1; 7:14-15), even though he also preached to Judah and the surrounding foreign nations. We might ask why God sent him to prophesy to the Northern Kingdom. James Robertson says the reason is not far to seek:

> It is the manner of the prophets to appear where they are most needed; and the Northern Kingdom about that time had come victorious out of war [2 K 14:25], and had reached its culmination of wealth and power, with the attendant results of luxury and excess, while the Southern Kingdom had been enjoying a period of outward tranquility and domestic content.[5]

The message God wanted to deliver to Israel was strong and severe, so God chose for His messenger a man who withstood the rigors of a disciplined life and who knew what hardness was. In the waste howling wildernesses around Tekoa, life was full of poverty and danger—it was an empty and silent world, very wild. Amos knew God, and he knew the Scriptures, even though he was not trained in the school of the prophets (7:14). This ideal preparation for the task was just as much of God as was his call. His prophetic ministry lasted for about ten years, 765-755 B.C.

3. Henrietta C. Mears, *What the Bible Is All About*, p. 288.
4. Comill, quoted by George Adam Smith, *The Book of the Twelve Prophets*, 1:71.
5. James Robertson, "Amos," in *The International Standard Bible Encyclopedia*, vol. 1, ed. James Orr (Grand Rapids: Eerdmans, 1952), p. 121.

## B. The Book of Amos

### 1. *Author and date*

Amos wrote this book toward the end of Jeroboam's reign, around 760 B.C. Most of the nine chapters are "the words" (i.e., messages or sermons) of Amos (1:1). One narrative section appears at 7:10-17.

Chart K shows Amos among his contemporaries. Study this carefully, to fix in your mind the historical setting of the book. What prophets of Israel ministered before and after Amos? What kings reigned over Israel and Judah during Amos's ministry? Compare 1:1.

Hebrew prophecy was entering its golden age of excellence when Amos came on the scene:

> After the earliest of the writing prophets, Obadiah, Joel and Jonah, had done their work, the stage was set for the appearance of the four great figures who dominated the scene from 755 to the opening of the seventh century: Amos, Hosea, Micah and Isaiah.[6]

Amos shines not only for *what* he said but *how* he said it. Concerning his picturesque style, Scroggie says, "In vigour, vividness, and simplicity of speech he was not surpassed by any of his successors."[7]

### 2. *Audience*

Amos's main audience was Israel, which politically and economically was at a zenith of power. The threat of war had eased, and business was booming. A spirit of self-sufficiency and complacency thrived on material prosperity. The rich were getting richer, and the poor were getting poorer. Idolatry, hypocrisy, moral corruption, and social injustices were everywhere. The nation was truly on the brink of disaster. In fact, on God's timetable, destruction was due in about three decades (722 B.C.). Such was the soul and destiny of the audience of Amos the prophet.

### 3. *Message*

Amos was not a popular prophet. This does not surprise us, for to most people he was a "calamity howler." His preaching was mainly stern denunciation, only because this was the message God gave him to deliver. When he likened the Lord to a roaring

---

6. Gleason L. Archer, *A Survey of Old Testament Introduction*, p. 304.
7. W. Graham Scroggie, *Know Your Bible* (London: Pickering & Inglis, 1940), 1:163.

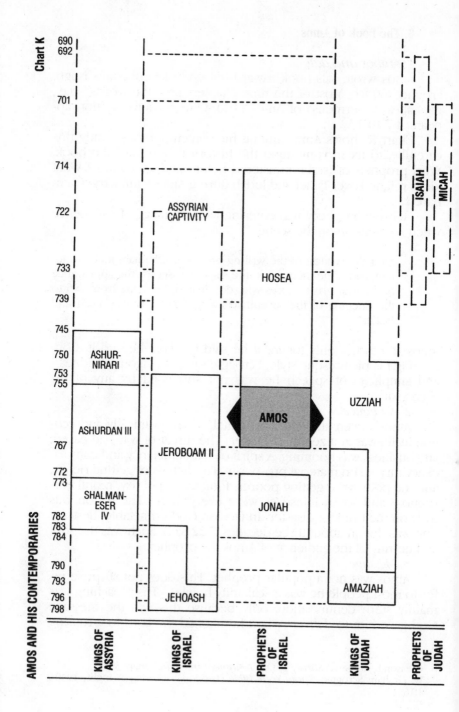

**Chart K**

**AMOS AND HIS CONTEMPORARIES**

| KINGS OF ASSYRIA | KINGS OF ISRAEL | PROPHETS OF ISRAEL | KINGS OF JUDAH | PROPHETS OF JUDAH |
|---|---|---|---|---|

690
692
701
714
722
733
739
745
750
753
755
767
772
773
782
783
784
790
793
796
798

ASHUR-NIRARI

ASHURDAN III

SHALMAN-ESER IV

JEROBOAM II

JEHOASH

ASSYRIAN CAPTIVITY

HOSEA

AMOS

JONAH

UZZIAH

AMAZIAH

ISAIAH

MICAH

48

lion, he wanted to impress upon his hearers the awfulness of sin and its judgment:

> The Lord will roar from Zion (1:2)
> The Lion hath roared, who will not fear? (3:8)

Amos's preaching was so sharp and vigorous that he was accused of sedition by Amaziah, idolatrous high priest of Bethel (7:10-17).

Like most prophets, Amos underscored these key truths:

(a) The people's sin

(b) The coming of judgment

(c) The righteousness and holiness of God

(d) The mercy of God in offering deliverance

The book has often been criticized as a "dark book." Do some situations in life call for "dark" books? It will be clear to us as we study the text that Amos's main purpose in stirring conviction of sin and repentance in the people was not to alleviate his own grief over their evil ways. Rather, he yearned that as individuals and as a nation they would come to a personal knowledge of God as their Lord. A key statement of his book is the Lord's gracious invitation:

> "SEEK YE ME, AND YE SHALL LIVE" (5:4).

### 4. Geography of Amos

Map 3, Geography of Amos, shows the geographical places that Amos cites in his messages. Amos was obviously well-versed in Palestinian history and geography, as indicated by such a large number of references. As you study the Bible text, refer to the map whenever you come upon a place name. You will find that the setting or action comes alive when you visualize. "To visualize is to empathize."

Not shown on the map are the following:

| Places Beyond the Limits of the Map | Locations Unknown[8] |
|---|---|
| Egypt<br>Ethiopia<br>Kir (1:5)<br>Hamath (6:2)<br>Calneh (6:2) | Sodom and Gomorrah<br>Caphtor (9:7)<br>Eden (1:5)<br>Teman (1:12) |

8. Present-day Sodom is located at the southern end of the Dead Sea. Refer to a Bible dictionary for suggested locations of the cities shown on the list.

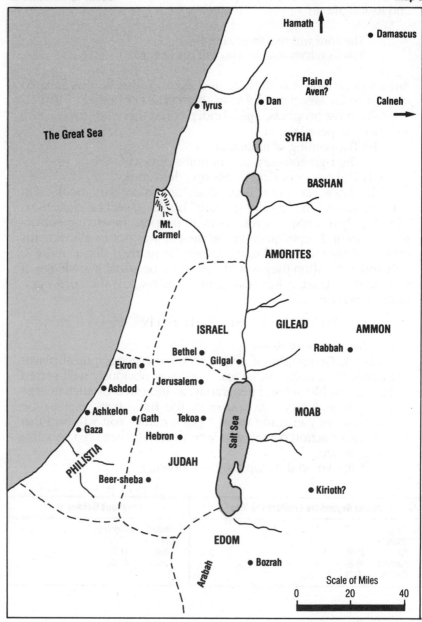

### 5. *New Testament quotes*

The book of Amos is quoted twice in the New Testament. Read the references listed below, comparing the Old Testament text and the New Testament quote:

| Book of Amos | New Testament |
|---|---|
| 5:25-27<br>9:11-12 | Acts 7:42-43 (Stephen's sermon)<br>Acts 15:16-17 (James, at the Jerusalem Council) |

## II. SURVEY

Now that we have learned the background of the book of Amos, let us begin to read its text. For the remainder of this lesson we will survey the book to see its general makeup, and then, beginning at Lesson 6, we will analyze its chapters in detail, which is the heart of Bible study.

### A. First Reading

Scan the book once or twice for overall impressions. Here are come things to look for in such a survey:

1. Overall tone (e.g., is the book severe, mellow, meditative, philosophical, practical?)

2. Tone of the opening chapters as compared with that of the closing verses (9:11-15)

3. Groupings of Amos's messages (e.g., beginning at 7:1 is a group of visions)

4. Repeated words and phrases

5. Verses that strike you, for whatever reason

### B. A Survey Chart

Chart L is a survey of the book of Amos, showing its structure and highlights. Observe the following on the chart:

1. The book has a short introduction (1:1-2) but no formal conclusion.

2. There are three types of writing:

(a) Lyric prophecy (ORACLES)—chapters 1-2
   Key repeated phrase: "Thus saith the Lord" (e.g., 1:3)

(b) Teaching discourse (SERMONS)—chapters 3-6
   Read the opening verse, 3:1.

(c) Dramatic revelation (VISIONS)—chapters 7-9
   Key repeated phrase: "The Lord God showed unto me" (e.g., 7:1)

51

# AMOS  PREPARE TO MEET GOD

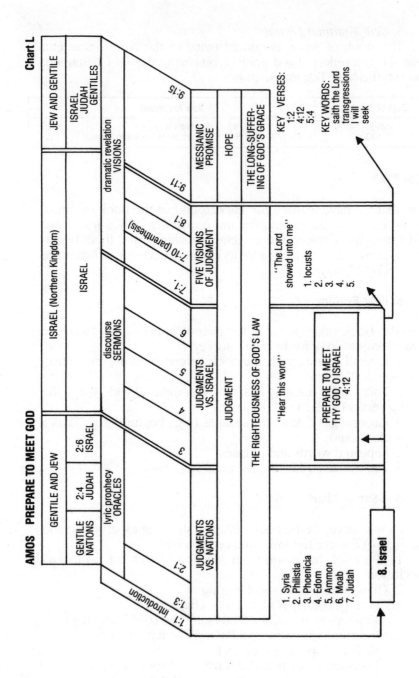

Chart L

| GENTILE AND JEW | | | ISRAEL (Northern Kingdom) | | | | JEW AND GENTILE |
|---|---|---|---|---|---|---|---|
| GENTILE NATIONS | 2:4 JUDAH | 2:6 ISRAEL | ISRAEL | | | | ISRAEL JUDAH GENTILES |

lyric prophecy ORACLES | discourse SERMONS | dramatic revelation VISIONS

1:1 Introduction | 1:3 | 2:1 | 3 | 4 | 5 | 6 | 7:1 | 7:10 (parenthesis) | 8:1 | 9:11 | 9:15

| JUDGMENTS VS. NATIONS | JUDGMENTS VS. ISRAEL | FIVE VISIONS OF JUDGMENT | MESSIANIC PROMISE |
|---|---|---|---|

| JUDGMENT | | | HOPE |

THE RIGHTEOUSNESS OF GOD'S LAW | | | THE LONG-SUFFER-ING OF GOD'S GRACE

"Hear this word" — "The Lord showed unto me"

PREPARE TO MEET THY GOD, O ISRAEL 4:12

1. Syria
2. Philistia
3. Phoenicia
4. Edom
5. Ammon
6. Moab
7. Judah

8. Israel

1. locusts
2.
3.
4.
5.

KEY VERSES:
1:2
4:12
5:4

KEY WORDS:
saith the Lord
transgressions
I will
seek

52

3. Most of the book is about judgment. What is the last section (9:11-15) about? What other two-point outline represents the book?

4. Four sections are clearly discernible in the book. Mark these in your Bible. Check the text to see the identifying phrases that mark the sections.

Judgments against the nations — chapters 1-2
Judgments against Israel    — chapters 3-6
Visions of judgment         — 7:1–9:10
Messianic promise           — 9:11-15

5. Study the two outlines at the top of Chart L, which identify the people whom Amos's messages are about. Read in your Bible the verses that support these identifications.

| | People | Message | Verses |
|---|---|---|---|
| GENTILE and JEW | Gentile Nations | 1:3–2:3 | 1:3, 6, 9, 11, 13; 2:1 |
| | Judah | 2:4-5 | 2:4 |
| | Israel | 2:6-16 | 2:6 |
| ISRAEL (Northern Kingdom) | Israel (mainly) | 3:1–9:10 | 7:10-17 (Note distinction between Israel and Judah.*) |
| JEW and GENTILE | Israel and Judah | 9:11-15 | 9:11, 14 (references fo chosen people of God) |
| | Gentiles | | 9:12 (''heathen'') |

6. Complete the listing of the five visions, beginning with locusts (''grasshoppers'').

7. As you proceed with your study, you may want to add to Chart L any references to deliverance and salvation that may appear in the text (e.g., at 5:4; the high point of this redemptive theme is the last section, 9:11-15.)

8. Note the key words and key verses. Add to these lists along the way.

* * *

## REVIEW QUESTIONS

1. How many things can you remember about the man Amos?

2. Had Amos been trained in the school of the prophets?

3. What aspects of Amos's background would explain (1) the many geographical references and (2) the many pictures from nature that are found in this book?

4. Which kings and prophets were Amos's contemporaries?

5. Amos was the first of four prophets of the golden age of excellence of Hebrew prophecy. Who were the other three?

6. Describe the people of Israel (Northern Kingdom) in Amos's day.

7. Why do you think God sent a native of Judah to prophesy to the people of Israel?

8. What were the four key truths of Amos's preaching?

9. What are the four main sections of the book of Amos?

10. What one word describes the content of most of the book?

11. Where is the bright messianic passage located in the book?

12. Quote one of the key verses of the book.

# Lesson 6

# The Nations' Transgressions

The oracles of these opening chapters apply the divine, universal, timeless principle that sin brings judgment. At no place in the Bible is this principle contradicted. God in His holiness cannot overlook or excuse the sin of anyone (Jew or Gentile) at any time (before Christ or after). If there were no judgment for sin, God would not be God. Further, utter chaos in the world would be inevitable, and men would not see their awful plight of being alienated from God eternally. God does not want chaos, nor does He want men to perish in their sins (2 Pet. 3:9). In fact this is where the gospel sounds forth—heralding the good news that when Christ died, He bore the judgment for the sins of all mankind, redeeming those who accept His gift of sacrifice (2 Cor. 5:15; John 3:18). Amos would never have been given the last vision of the book about future glory for Israel were it not for that forthcoming great event at Calvary.

## I. PREPARATION FOR STUDY

1. Review the survey Chart L and observe what chapters 1-2 contribute to the whole of the book. Note a progression leading up to Israel and then an amplification of the subject of Israel.

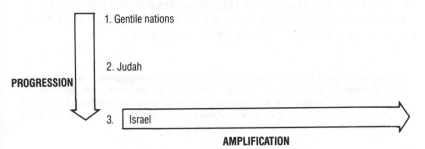

PROGRESSION

1. Gentile nations

2. Judah

3. Israel

AMPLIFICATION

2. Review the survey study you made in Lesson 5 concerning the people involved in the message of Amos (e.g., Gentile and Jew).

3. Look again at Map 3, Geography of Amos. Find the cities of Damascus, Gaza, and Tyrus (Tyre). What regions are they located in? Find also the regions of Edom, Ammon, Moab, Judah, and Israel.

4. Read Zechariah 14:5, which refers back to the historical event of the earthquake that Amos mentions in 1:1. It must have been a severe earthquake, to be singled out from among the many that occurred in those times.

## II. ANALYSIS

*Segment to be analyzed*: 1:1–2:16
*Paragraph divisions*[1]: at verses 1:1, 3, 6, 9, 11, 13; 2:1, 4, 6

### A. General Analysis

1. After you have marked the paragraph divisions in your Bible, read through the entire segment. What are the repeated words and phrases?

_____

_____

_____

How much is duplicated from oracle to oracle?

_____

2. What is the main theme of this passage?

_____

3. Chart M shows the order of paragraphs in this segment. Record in the oblique spaces the geographical name that appears in each paragraph after the words "for three transgressions of" (example is given). Note: The city of Damascus represents the country of Syria; Gaza represents Philistia; and Tyrus, Phoenicia.[2] Mark these regions in your Bible at the appropriate places.

---

1. Because of the book's lyric style, a more accurate designation would be "stanza divisions." However, this manual will stay with the paragraph designation. (NASB prints the book of Amos in stanza format, which is a big help for study.)
2. This figure of speech of using a *part* to designate the *whole* is called *synecdoche*.

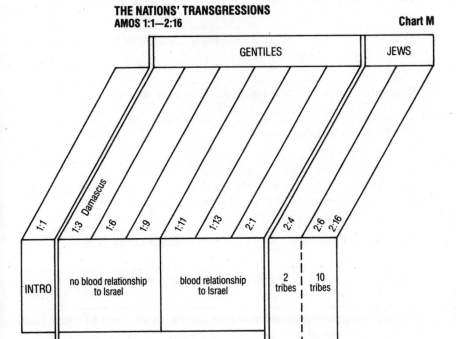

**THE NATIONS' TRANSGRESSIONS**
AMOS 1:1—2:16

Chart M

GENTILES | JEWS

1:1

1:3 Damascus

1:6

1:9

1:11

1:13

2:1

2:4

2:6

2:16

INTRO | no blood relationship to Israel | blood relationship to Israel | 2 tribes | 10 tribes

THE LORD WILL ROAR

1:2

## B. Paragraph Analysis

1. *Introductory paragraph: 1:1-2*
What does this phrase tell you: "The words of Amos . . . which he saw" (1:1)?

_____

_____

Note the reference to "the earthquake" (1:1). Amos saw his visions *before* the earthquake. Did he write the book *after* the earthquake? If so, at least how much time elapsed between the visions and the writing?

_____

What words of verse 2 would you consider to be key words?

How does this verse set the tone for the theme of the book? (Cf. a key phrase shown on Chart M.)

Why is the Lord identified with Zion and Jerusalem?

Where is His throne today?

2. *Transgressions of the Gentile nations: 1:3–2:3*
What kind of judgment did the Lord prophesy would fall upon all the Gentile nations? ("But I will send . . .")

Why do God's judgments often come in the form of fire?

What does the word "because" introduce in each oracle?

Record the different transgressions on the work sheet of Chart N.
    All but one of the cited transgressions of the Gentile nations were against God's chosen people.[3] Sometimes the offense is explicitly named in the text (e.g., "threshed Gilead," 1:3); otherwise it is only implied. The covenant blessings that God promised His chosen people included protection from harm by the surrounding heathen nations.

3. *Transgressions of Judah: 2:4-5*
What was Judah's underlying sin? (Read 2 Kings 17:13-18.)

At 2:5 Amos clearly prophesied the fall of Jerusalem, which came in 586 B.C., almost 200 years later. Read 2 Kings 25:8-11 for the reporting of this calamity. Did Judah (as well as Israel) have more spiritual light given to them than the Gentile nations?

How are light and responsibility related in God's accounting? See Luke 12:47-48.

---

3. The exception is that of 2:1.

AMOS 1:3—2:3

| Country | Historical record | Amos's words | Your summary |
|---|---|---|---|
| Syria | 2 Kings 8:12-13<br><br>2 Kings 10:32-33 | 1:3 | |
| Philistia | 2 Chron. 21:16-17<br><br>2 Chron. 28:18 | 1:6 | |
| Phoenicia | 1 Kings 5:12<br><br>(cf. Joel 3:6-7) | 1:9 | |
| Edom | 2 Chron. 21:8-10<br><br>2 Kings 8:20-22 | 1:11 | |
| Ammon | 2 Kings 8:12<br><br>2 Kings 10:32-33 | 1:13 | |
| Moab | 2 Kings 3:27 | 2:1 | |

## 4. *Transgressions of Israel: 2:6-16*
In what ways does this oracle differ from the preceding ones?

Since Amos was preaching particularly to Israel, what may his listeners have been thinking as he described God's indictments against the Gentile nations and against Judah?

Was it appropriate for him to speak in more detail about Israel than about Judah? (Recall that the indictment against Judah was brief and broad, 2:4.)

Read 2 Kings 17:20-23 for a brief summary of Israel's sins. Read verses 9-12 as a unit. What had the Lord done for Israel, and what was their response? ("I . . . but ye.")

What sins does Amos cite in verses 6-8, 12?

What point does Amos repeat many times in verses 14-16?

Is the event of "that day" one of those shown on Chart M?

## III. NOTES

For background to the many geographical and historical references of Amos's prophecies, consult a commentary and compare the readings of modern paraphrases.

1. *"For three transgressions . . . and for four"* (1:3). This was a Jewish idiom meaning "for multiplied sins." The Hebrew word translated "transgressions" means literally rebellion or revolt. The Gentiles were just as guilty of rebellion against God as the disobedient Jews were.

2. *"Threshed Gilead"* (1:3). The bodies of the people were literally thrashed and ripped (2 Kings 8:12-13).

3. *"I will send a fire"* (1:4). Fire symbolized war, since fire was a common weapon in war. Compare 2:5 with 2 Kings 25:9.

4. *"His brother"* (1:11; cf. Deut. 2:4; 23:7.) Edom and Israel were descended from the brothers Esau and Jacob, respectively. So Edom "did pursue his brother" Israel. (Cf. Num. 20:17-21.)

5. *"I am pressed under you"* (2:13). The Lord was deeply grieved over the sins of His people. (Cf. Isa. 43:24.) Some versions translate this verse as meaning God's judgments will curse His people. (See *Berkeley; American Standard Version.*)

## IV. FOR THOUGHT AND DISCUSSION

1. Why do you think God often used war as an instrument of His judgment in Old Testament times? Do you think He uses the same instrument today? Does the book of Revelation describe wars and judgments, under His sovereign control, as taking place in last times?

2. Why is fire often a part of God's judgment? Read Revelation 20:10, 14-15 and note the prophecies of eternal fire. Is that kind of fire meant to purify? How would you answer the contention of those who say that the fires of hell are to purge and refine and that therefore condemned sinners will be eventually delivered from hell?

3. Two basic attributes of God are love and holiness. Are both of these manifested in Old Testament history? What references to God's grace did you read in the passage of this lesson? How is God's love related to His holiness? Do they contradict each other?

4. People of Judah "despised the law of the Lord" (2:4). Is this sin committed today by unbelievers? Can it be committed by backslidden Christians? If so, in what ways?

5. Amos prophesied judgments upon nations that were fulfilled before too long. What books of the New Testament prophesy especially about events yet to take place?

## V. FURTHER STUDY

1. You may want to spend more time analyzing the meaning of phrases of this passage that are tied in with geography (e.g., "the bar of Damascus," 1:5). Commentaries and modern versions will be of much help in this.

2. Read 1 Kings 12 for the historical record of the split of the kingdom, which took place in 931 B.C. (See Chart A.) Here are the three main parts of that key chapter:

12:1-20   Events leading up to the split
12:21-24  The new kingdom of Judah, under King Rehoboam
12:25-33  The new kingdom of Israel, under King Jeroboam

## VI. WORDS TO PONDER

The Lord says, "The people of Israel have sinned again and again, and I will not forget it" (Amos 2:6, *The Living Bible*)

# Lesson 7

# Judgments Against Israel

The chapters studied in this lesson are the core of Amos's preaching to the Northern Kingdom of Israel. All the sermons are woven around the basic principle of *cause* and *effect* (sin brings judgment), which we saw also in the oracles of the first two chapters. Sinners outside the family of God do not like to think about God as the Holy One—they would rather contend that His holiness is swallowed up by His love.[1] But no sinner reaps the eternal fruit of God's love if his sins have not been reckoned with first according to the holy judgments of God. (Calvary was crucial.) Amos preached to Israel that sin (cause) brings judgment (effect). Judgment is inevitable. But even though most of Amos's words were about judgment, he also magnified the grace and mercy of God. Only in God are the two ingredients of judgment and mercy perfectly combined. (Read Ps. 85:10.)

## I. PREPARATION FOR STUDY

1. This lesson covers a long Bible text—eight and one-half chapters, so you will want to study it in more than one unit. After you have studied Chart O, you will be able to determine how you want to approach the passage. (For example, three study units could be: 3:1–4:13; 5:1–6:14; 7:1–9:10.)

2. Recall how the first two chapters of Amos recognize God as sovereign over all (see following diagram).

The passage of this lesson sometimes involves foreign nations (e.g., 5:27), and the message is even directed to Judah at

---

1. This is the foundation doctrine of *agape* theologians, who hold the universalist view that all people will be saved, since God loves all.

times (cf. 3:1). But for the most part Amos is preaching to the kingdom of Israel in the north.[2] (See 7:12, 15.)

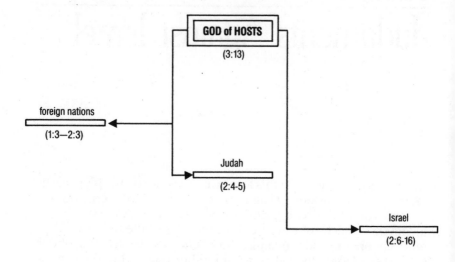

3. Read the biographical account of 7:10-17, to sense the cold-hearted reception given Amos for his preaching. How did he validate his message?

4. Have available a modern version or paraphrase to aid you in understanding unclear verses of the King James Version (e.g., 4:3).

## II. ANALYSIS

*Segments to be analyzed:* 3:1-8; 3:9–4:3; 4:4-13; 5:1-27; 6:1-14; 7:1-9; 7:10-17; 8:1-14; 9:1-10.

*Paragraph divisions:* 3:1, 9, 11; 4:1, 4, 6, 12; 5:1, 4, 8, 10, 14, 16, 18, 21; 6:1, 7, 12; 7:1, 4, 7, 10; 8:1, 4, 7, 11; 9:1, 5, 8. Mark these paragraph divisions in your Bible. Do not let such a long passage intimidate you as you begin your study. This manual will help you keep the "forest" in view as you look at the many "trees."

---

2. In the Old Testament the name Israel sometimes refers to God's chosen people as a whole (e.g., 3:1), and sometimes it refers to only the northern ten tribes (e.g., 7:10). The rule of thumb to follow in studying Amos is to take "Israel" to mean the Northern Kingdom unless there is clear indication otherwise. The spiritual application in either case generally remains the same.

## A. General Analysis

1. Study the main features of Chart O. Then scan the Bible text and keep referring to the chart to justify each part of an outline that is shown. For example, when you scan 6:1-6, see why this is represented on the chart as Sin of Ease. This exercise will give you a good overall view of the passage.

2. What outline divides the passage into three parts? Account for the following three outline words, on the basis of the verses cited:

|  |  |
|---|---|
| INDICTMENTS | (3:1) |
| LAMENTATIONS | (5:1) |
| VISIONS | (7:1) |

3. Three laws of composition are prominent in the passage. Note how these are shown on the chart:

REFLECTION—This shows up in the duo of cause and effect.
REPETITION—How often does the cause-effect theme
               appear?
PROGRESSION—Follow the arrow beginning at 7:1.

4. Note that the biographical passage 7:10-17 is a parenthesis in the midst of the five visions. Read 7:9 and 7:11 to see why the parenthesis appears at this place.

5. Read 9:8-10. Observe the ray of hope for a remnant. How is this represented on the chart?

## B. Segment Analysis

1. *Introductory Segment: 3:1-8*
These opening verses introduce two main themes that are developed in the remainder of the section:
*The principle of cause and effect.* What word in 3:2 represents cause, and what word represents effect?

_____

How does each of the examples of verses 3-7 illustrate this principle? (See *Notes* on verse 3.)

_____

_____

_____

_____

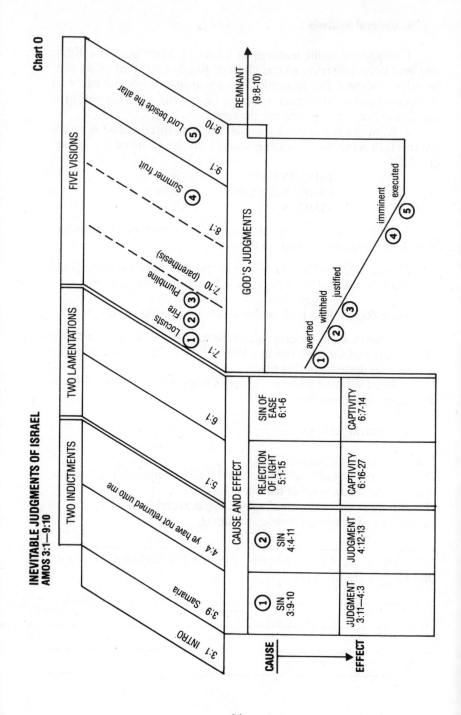

**INEVITABLE JUDGMENTS OF ISRAEL**
AMOS 3:1—9:10

Chart 0

**FIVE VISIONS**

| | | |
|---|---|---|
| 5 Lord beside the altar 9:10 | | |
| 4 Summer fruit 9:1 | | |
| 8:1 | | |

**GOD'S JUDGMENTS**

1 Locusts 7:1
2 Fire
3 Plumbline 7:10 (parenthesis)

REMNANT (9:8-10)

averted 1
withheld 2
justified 3
imminent 4
executed 5

**TWO LAMENTATIONS**

6:1

**TWO INDICTMENTS**

4:4 ye have not returned unto me
5:1

3:9 Samaria
3:1 INTRO

**CAUSE AND EFFECT**

| CAUSE | 1 SIN 3:9-10 | 2 SIN 4:4-11 | REJECTION OF LIGHT 5:1-15 | SIN OF EASE 6:1-6 |
|---|---|---|---|---|
| EFFECT | JUDGMENT 3:11—4:3 | JUDGMENT 4:12-13 | CAPTIVITY 6:16-27 | CAPTIVITY 6:7-14 |

How does 3:8 apply this cause-effect principle?

_The mandate that God gave the prophet._ What words clearly reveal that mandate? Compare 8:1*a* with 1:2.

## 2. _Two indictments: 3:9—4:4-13_

The key word that connects cause and effect in chapters 3-6 is "therefore." Underline in your Bible its two appearances in the two indictments. Record below, in summary form, the sins and the judgments of each indictment. (Note: Sometimes in the Bible text, sins are mentioned in the judgments section, and vice versa.)

|  | **First Indictment** | **Second Indictment** |
|---|---|---|
| **SINS** | 3:9-10 | 4:4-11 |
| **JUDGMENTS** | 3:11—4:3  "Therefore" | 4:12-13  "Therefore" |

Does it seem that 4:4-5 is meant to be read as irony, in view of the first few phrases of verse 4? (Compare _The Living Bible._)

What key phrase of seven words is repeated in 4:4-11?

Is the attribute of divine grace implied by the phrase?

What is the climactic statement of 4:13?

## 3. _Two lamentations: 5:1-27 and 6:1-14_

Such repeated words as "lamentation" (5:1) and "woe" (6:1) suggest the intense tone of this section. Again, Amos follows the theme of cause and effect, the latter being introduced by the word "therefore."

(a) *Cause* (5:1-15). How is Israel pictured in the opening paragraph (5:1-3)?

_____

_____

Compare this with the repeated invitations to "seek" in verses 4-15. Did Amos seem to know that Israel would persist in her sins? What are some of the sins mentioned here?

_____

_____

Compare "Seek ye me" (5:4) and "seek not Bethel" (5:5). Relate the latter phrase to your earlier interpretation of "Come to Bethel" at 4:4.

_____

_____

(b) *Effect* (5:16-27). Note that the opening word is "therefore" (5:16), and the closing reference is to sure captivity (5:27). When was the prophecy "captivity beyond Damascus" fulfilled? See Chart L. Note the repetition of "day of the Lord" in 5:18-20. What is taught here about that day?

_____

Compare 5:21-23 with 4:4-5. What attributes of God are exalted in 5:24?

_____

_____

_____

(c) *Cause* (6:1-6). The word "ease" (v. 1) is the key word of this paragraph. Compare the first line of 6:1 with the last line of 6:6.

_____

_____

Draw a line in your Bible connecting the two indictments. How do verses 6:1-6 describe the reckless and apathetic life of Judah ("Zion") and Israel ("Samaria")? Refer to a modern version for help in interpreting some of the verses. Also see Notes.

*(d) Effect* (6:7-14). What is the first word of verse 7?

_____

How does it introduce this paragraph?

_____

_____

What verses prophesy the judgment of captivity?

_____

What sins are described in verses 12-13?

_____

Read these verses also in a modern version.

### 4. *Five Visions: 7:1–9:10*

God gave five visions to Amos to impress him with the awesome dimensions of the impending judgments threatening the people of Israel.[3] How would the experience of seeing such visions help Amos to communicate the message of judgment to the people?

_____

_____

What was one reaction to his strong preaching, as recorded in 7:10-15?

_____

Refer to Chart O and observe the sequence of the five visions. Note the parenthesis of 7:10-17. Compare 7:9 and 7:11 in your Bible to see why Amos reported this confrontation after recording the vision of the plumbline.

Read the five visions of 7:1–9:10 and record observations on the work sheet of Chart P. (Examples are given.) What visions moved Amos to intercede for the people?

_____

_____

How does a plumbline work? (Consult a Bible dictionary if necessary.)

_____

_____

What was Amos mainly trying to get across by his testimony of 7:14-15? Compare 7:16 with 7:15.

_____

_____

_____

3. God frequently used audio-visual methods to reveal His message to His prophets. Compare the vision of figs given to Jeremiah (Jer. 24:1-10).

69

| Reference | Object of Vision | Description of Judgment | Progression of Judgment | Amos's Part |
|---|---|---|---|---|
| 7:1-3 | LOCUSTS ("grass-hoppers") | spring crop destroyed | judgment averted | intercession |
| 4-6 | FIRE | | judgment withheld | |
| 7-9 | PLUMBLINE | | judgment justified | |
| 8:1-14 | SUMMER FRUIT | | judgment imminent | |
| 9:1-10 | LORD BESIDE THE ALTAR | | judgment executed | |

The summer fruit was the fully ripe harvest of the late summer or early autumn. In what way does it symbolize the imminency of judgment?[4]

What is the main truth of 9:1-7? Note that 9:1-4 is mainly about judgment, whereas 9:5-7 is mainly about God, who executes the judgment. Compare the dark picture of 9:1-7 with that of 9:8-10. Of these latter verses, one has written, "The dark, dark sky has a few stars." Read the following references to preservation of a Jewish remnant: Amos 5:15; Isaiah 1:9; 10:22; 11:11; Micah 2:12; 4:7; Romans 9:27-29. (This subject will be studied further in the next lesson.)

### III. NOTES

1. *"Can two walk together"* (3:3). An accurate translation of the phrase that follows these words is "unless they have made an appointment" (NASB). The illustrations of 3:3-7 are about the unlikelihood of *effect* without *cause*.[5] For example, it is unlikely that two men walking in the wilderness would be together (effect) unless by prior planning (cause).

2. *"Come to Bethel"* (4:4). Bethel (*beth-*"house"; *el-*"God") was one of the two cities that Jeroboam I designated as national centers of worship for the Northern Kingdom (1 Kings 12:26-30). (Jerusalem was the "holy city" of the Southern Kingdom.)

3. *"Calneh...Hamath...Gath"* (6:2). These three foreign cities were once great but had since fallen. Calneh was located in the east, around Mesopotamia; Hamath in the north, on the Orontes River; and Gath in the south, in Philistia.

4. *"The evil day"* (6:3). This is better translated as "the day of calamity." See *The Living Bible* for a good paraphrase of the entire verse.

5. *"God hath sworn by himself"* (6:8). For clarification of this phrase, compare these verses: Hebrews 6:13; Amos 4:2; Jeremiah 51:14; Genesis 22:16.

6. *"Excellency of Jacob"* (6:8). NASB translates this as "arrogance of Jacob."

---

4. It is interesting to observe a play on words in the Hebrew text. The word for "summer fruit," *qayits*, sounds much like the word for "end," *qatseh*. See "the end is come" in 8:2.)

5. The illustration of 3:7 fits this context when the phrase "but he revealeth" reads "unless He has revealed" *(New Berkeley)*.

7. *"Ye have turned judgment into gall"* (6:12). A clearer translation is "You have turned justice into poison" (NASB).

8. *"River of the wilderness"* (6:14). This should read "brook of the Arabah." This is a reference to the geological depression south of the Dead Sea. Amos's prophecy of affliction from Hamath to Arabah (6:14) means therefore from the north to the south.

9. *"Hell"* (9:2). The word "hell" translates the Hebrew *sheol* in all of the thirty-one verses of the King James Old Testament. Sheol was the abode of the spirits of the deceased: unbelievers and believers. The region assigned to unbelievers was a place of torment, whereas that of believers was one of blessedness.[6]

10. *"Have not I brought up . . . the Philistines from Caphtor, and the Syrians from Kir?"* (9:7). God is sovereign over all nations of the world, not only His chosen nation.

## IV. FOR THOUGHT AND DISCUSSION

1. Someone has written, "A man does not choose to be a prophet; he is chosen." How does this truth apply to Amos? See 1:1; 3:8; 7:14-15. Does it apply to Christian workers today?

2. Is there hope for a people when their religious leader is a false shepherd? Recall the story of Amaziah, the priest of Bethel (7:10-17).

3. Evaluate this statement: "Every prophecy of judgment is an invitation to repentance."[7] What do you think is meant by the words "Prepare to meet thy God, O Israel" (4:12b)? Are they a warning; a call to repentance; or both?

4. Write a list of various spiritual lessons taught by 3:1–9:10. Apply these to your own life, whenever they are so intended.

## V. FURTHER STUDY

1. With the help of outside sources[8] study what the Bible says about these subjects: holiness, righteousness, judgment, remnant of believers.

---

6. See Merrill F. Unger, *Unger's Bible Dictionary* (Chicago: Moody, 1957), p. 1012.

7. Arnold Schultz, "Amos," in *The Wycliffe Bible Commentary*, p. 834.

8. Suggested aids are: an exhaustive concordance, a Bible dictionary or Bible encyclopedia, a book on doctrine, and a book of word and topical studies (e.g., *Nave's Topical Bible.*).

2. You may want to study how Stephen, one of the early church's leaders, applied Amos 5:26-27 in his sermon recorded in Acts. See Acts 7:42-43.[9]

## VI. WORDS TO PONDER

Behold, the days come, saith the Lord God, that I WILL SEND A FAMINE in the land, not a famine of bread, nor a thirst for water, but OF HEARING THE WORDS OF THE LORD: and THEY SHALL WANDER from sea to sea, and from the north even to the east, THEY SHALL RUN to and fro TO SEEK THE WORD OF THE LORD, AND SHALL NOT FIND IT (Amos 8:11-12, emphasis added).

9. For help on this Acts passage, see F. F. Bruce, *Commentary on the Book of Acts* (Grand Rapids: Eerdmans, 1954), pp. 140, 153-56.

# Lesson 8

# The Final Restoration

**T**he brightest vision given to any of the Old Testament prophets was of Israel's restoration to glory. Most of the book of Amos is dark and tragic. But its last five verses quote the Lord's promise to restore Israel in the last days and to establish a kingdom unparalleled in her history. This is the subject of our present lesson.

## I. PREPARATION FOR STUDY

1. Recall from your study of the last lesson that God promised not to "utterly destroy the house of Jacob" (9:8). In other words, there would always be at least a remnant of believing Jews on the stage of world history. Simeon and Anna are two examples of believing Jews living at the time of Jesus' birth (Luke 2:25-38). Read 2 Samuel 7:8-17 and observe that God promised to "stablish the throne of his [David's] kingdom *for ever*" (v. 13). This is the irrevocable time reference of the messianic kingdom.

2. Read Joel 3:18-21 and Micah 4:1-8 for other prophecies similar to the passage of this lesson. Note that Micah 4:1 assigns the fulfillment of the prophecies to "the last days." In the premillennial scheme of events these passages describe the Millennium, when Christ will reign over all the earth on the throne of David. The millennial blessings will be the joys of Israel especially.

3. Recognize the possibility of multiple fulfillment in Bible prophecies. For example, the words "In that day will I raise up the tabernacle of David" (9:11) could refer to both immediate restoration of Israel's worship (after the Assyrian and Babylonian captivities) *and* ultimate restoration in the last days (1 and 2 on Chart Q).

4. Read Acts 15:1-17 and note how James applied Amos 9:11-12 to the situation discussed at the Jerusalem Council.

74

# TWO PROPHESIED JUDGMENTS AND RESTORATIONS OF ISRAEL

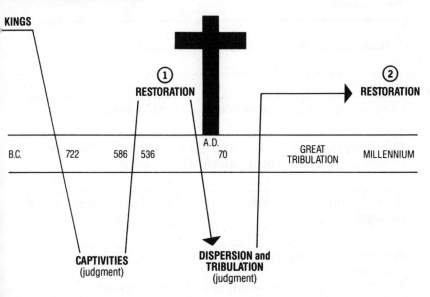

## II. ANALYSIS

*Segment to be analyzed*: 9:11-15
*Paragraph divisions*: at verse 13

1. Read verses 11-12. According to 9:11, what things does God promise to do for Israel?[1]

Compare similar prophecies in Jeremiah 24:6; 32:40-41; 42:10-12.
2. According to 9:12, what is a main purpose or fruit of God's restoring work?

Keep in mind that Edom was one of Israel's ancient enemies. (Read Ps. 137:7 in the context of the whole psalm.) Do you see both a near and long-range fulfillment suggested by the prophecy? Record your conclusions:

1. This last prophecy of Amos (9:11-15) does not distinguish between the Northern Kingdom (Israel) and the Southern Kingdom (Judah).

75

| PROPHECY | NEAR FULFILLMENT | LONG-RANGE FULFILLMENT |
|---|---|---|
| "they may possess. . . ." | | |

3. What conditions are described in verses 13-14?

_____

_____

How permanent a restoration is suggested by verse 15?

_____

Has Israel ever been "pulled up out of their land" since the days of return from Babylonian captivity (c. 536 B.C.)?

_____

If so, is a long-range fulfillment (in the last days) suggested by the passage?

_____

For similar prophecies of permanent blessing, read 2 Samuel 7:10; Isaiah 60:21; Joel 3:20.
4. What are the last five words of the book of Amos?

_____

Compare them with the opening words of 1:1.

_____

_____

What are your reflections?

_____

_____

### III. NOTES

1. *"Heathen"* (9:12). This may be read as "nations" or "Gentiles." (See NASB.) In the millennial kingdom Christ's reign will be universal, extending to Gentile as well as to Jew. Read Galatians 3:14 to see how Jew and Gentile are brought together.

2. *"Their land which I have given them"* (9:15). The permanent deed to the land of Israel was originally executed when God raised up Abraham to be the father of the chosen people. Read Genesis 17:8.

76

3. *"I will bring again the captivity"* (9:14). The *New Berkeley Version* reads, "I will turn the captivity." A paraphrase might read, "I will restore the fortunes."

## IV. FOR THOUGHT AND DISCUSSION

1. Can the modern state of Israel claim legal ownership of Palestine? Justify your answer.

2. One of the amazing phenomena of current events is the continual return of Jews to Palestine from all over the world. The Jewish population there has quadrupled since 1948, year of the revival of the state of Israel. In 1970 there were 2,561,400 Jews living in Palestine.[2] Jews are not returning as believers in Christ, but they are returning. How is the stage being set for the end-times fulfillment of Old Testament prophecies of Israel's eventually worshiping Jesus as their Messiah (Christ)?

3. How do you view the ongoing process of world history as it relates to God? Is God sovereign over nations as well as individuals?

4. Where will all human history eventually culminate?

5. What do you learn about the grace of God from the passage of this lesson?

6. Think back over the book of Amos. What are the prominent spiritual truths that you have studied in the book?

## V. FURTHER STUDY

You may want to make an extended study of the restoration of Israel in the last times as taught by such books as Ezekiel. (See *Ezekiel-Daniel*, pp. 40-49, of this self-study series, for help in this. Also refer to commentaries.)

## VI. WORDS TO PONDER

The time will come when . . . I will restore the fortunes of my people Israel (Amos 9:13-14, *The Living Bible*).

---

2. *Facts About Israel 1972* (Israel: Keter, 1972), p. 42.

# Lesson 9
# Background and Survey of Hosea

**H**osea was the last writing prophet to minister to Israel before they fell to the Assyrians in 722 B.C. He has been called the prophet of "Israel's zero hour" because "the nation had sunk to a point of such corruption that a major stroke of Divine judgment could no longer be staved off."[1] But even though judgment is a main subject of Hosea's message, the book is remembered mostly for its vivid pictures of the love and grace of God. Someone has well remarked, "There is nothing of divine grace that is not found in the book of Hosea." Your study of this inspired Scripture should lead you into a deeper knowledge of who God is and how He deals with sinners.

## I. BACKGROUND

You will better understand and appreciate the message of Hosea if you can learn what caused it to be written in the first place. So the studies of this lesson introduce first the man Hosea and then the book he wrote.

### A. The Man Hosea

1. *Name*
The name Hosea (Heb., *Hoshea*) means "salvation." It is interesting to observe that the names *Joshua* (Num. 13:16) and *Jesus* (Matt. 1:21) are derived from the same Hebrew root as Hosea.
2. *Family and home*
Hosea's father was named Beeri (1:1). We do not know what Beeri's occupation was. He may have been a middle-class merchant or even a farmer or cattle raiser. Hosea used many illustra-

1. J. Sidlow Baxter, *Explore the Book* (Grand Rapids: Zondervan, 1966), 4:89.

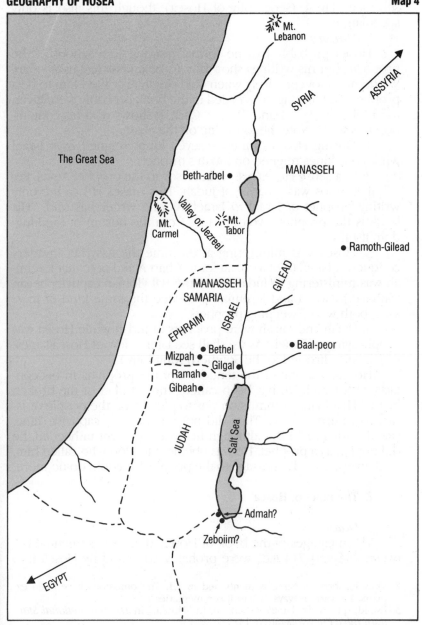

tions of agricultural settings when he wrote, which suggests that the prophet lived close to the soil in his young life. (Cf. 4:16; 6:4; 10:12.) His home may have been in a town of Ephraim or Manasseh (see Map 4, Geography of Hosea), though this also is only speculation.

### 3. Ministry

Hosea probably had no formal training in a school of the prophets, but his writings show him to be a knowledgeable man. We do not know precisely when God originally called him to be a prophet. The messages recorded in the book probably were given to him between 754 and 714 B.C. Chart R shows who his contemporaries were. Note the following on the chart:

1. During Hosea's ministry seven kings reigned over Israel while four kings reigned on Judah's throne.[2]

2. In a sense Hosea was a successor to the prophet Amos. Recall that Amos was a native of Judah. This makes Hosea the only writing prophet *of* Israel *to* Israel. As one writer has said, "His book is the prophetic voice wrung from the bosom of the kingdom itself."[3]

3. Hosea was ministering at the time the Assyrian invaders conquered Israel (722 B.C.).[4] Refer to Chart A and note that Jeremiah was ministering to Judah when the Babylonian captivity began (586 B.C.). Hosea and Jeremiah preached the same kind of message; both were "weeping prophets."

4. Isaiah and Micah were prophets of Judah while Hosea was prophesying to Israel. (As we shall see later, a few of Hosea's messages were directed to the Southern Kingdom.)

Hosea was one of the tenderest of the prophets in his contacts with Israel. He has been called "the prophet of the broken heart." His divine commission was to plead with the people of Israel to return to God. They did not respond, so captivity came. (Read 2 Kings 17.) But although his message went unheeded, he did not fail as a prophet. He was obedient to God who called him, by delivering God's message to the people. He could do no more.

### B. The Book of Hosea

### 1. Date

The messages of the book of Hosea, delivered sometime between 754 and 714 B.C., were probably compiled by Hosea into

---

2. Only Jeroboam's name is mentioned in 1:1. The omissions have been explained in various ways. (Consult commentaries.)
3. Ewald, quoted by James Robertson, in "Hosea," in *The International Standard Bible Encyclopedia*, p. 1425.
4. Some think that Hosea moved to Judah at the time of the conquest.

one book toward the end of that period. Gleason Archer suggests 725 B.C. as a possible date.[5] If that is so, Hosea completed the book before the Assyrian captivity (722 B.C.). That judgment was foretold in the book, not reported as having already taken place.

## 2. Setting

In the days of Hosea the Northern Kingdom politically was plagued by anarchy, unrest, and confusion. The quick succession of kings (Chart R) suggests such an instability. One political faction favored alliance with Egypt; another, with Assyria. One writer comments on 7:11 thus: "Israel was like a silly dove . . . fluttering everywhere but to God."[6] Economically the nation was prosperous. Spiritually this was the darkest hour of Israel. Idolatry, immorality, and haughty rejection of God's love spelled disaster. Israel was a backslidden people when Hosea preached to them (14:4). Read 2 Kings 15-17 to sense how black the darkness was.

## 3. Theme

The theme of Hosea is this: The tender-loving God offers one last chance of restoration to hard-hearted, adulterous Israel. Israel is the unfaithful wife who has deserted her husband and gone after other lovers. God through the prophet Hosea invites her back: "O Israel, return unto the Lord thy God" (14:1). (Read these passages about God's love: 2:14, 15, 19, 20; chap. 3; 11:3, 4, 8; chap. 14; cf. Rom. 11:22.) Hosea could be called the prophet of love in the Old Testament.

## 4. Language and style

Hosea's style is abrupt, short, and sharp ("he flashes forth brilliant sentences"). But tenderness is the book's prevailing tone. Scroggie says, "His message is one of the most profound and spiritual in the Old Testament."[7] The authoritarian tone is heard throughout the book, even though the familiar declaration "[Thus] saith the Lord" appears only four times. Symbols and metaphors abound, the prominent one being that of marriage (chaps. 1-3). The messages of chapters 4 to 14 were apparently not compiled with an outline in mind. Transitions are hard to detect because they are submerged in the emotional makeup of the book. As one writer observes, "The sentences fall from him like the sobs of a broken heart."[8]

5. Gleason L. Archer, *A Survey of Old Testament Introduction*, p. 310.
6. E. Heavenor, "Hosea" in *The New Bible Dictionary*, ed. J. D. Douglas, p. 539.
7. W. Graham Scroggie, *Know Your Bible* 1:166.
8. James Robertson, "Hosea," in *The International Standard Bible Encyclopedia*, p. 1426.

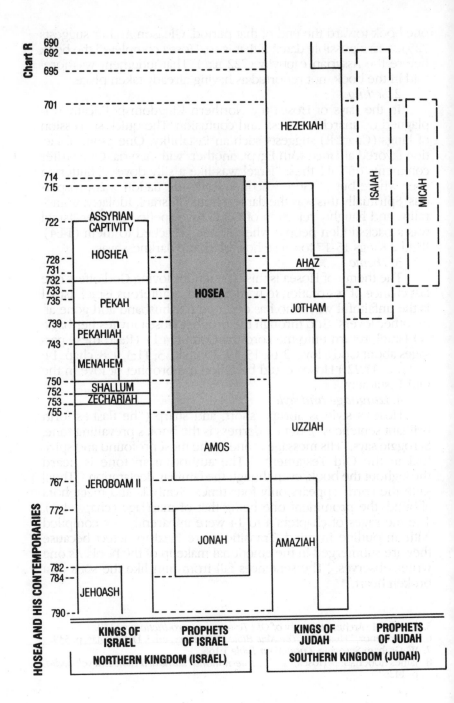

**Chart R**

**HOSEA AND HIS CONTEMPORARIES**

| | | | |
|---|---|---|---|
| | | 690 | |
| | | 692 | |
| | | 695 | |
| | | 701 | |
| | HEZEKIAH | | ISAIAH / MICAH |
| | | 714 | |
| | | 715 | |
| ASSYRIAN CAPTIVITY | | 722 | |
| HOSHEA | | 728 | AHAZ |
| | | 731 | |
| | HOSEA | 732 | |
| PEKAH | | 733 | JOTHAM |
| | | 735 | |
| PEKAHIAH | | 739 | |
| MENAHEM | | 743 | |
| SHALLUM | | 750 | |
| ZECHARIAH | | 752 | |
| | | 753 | |
| | | 755 | UZZIAH |
| JEROBOAM II | AMOS | 767 | |
| | | 772 | |
| | JONAH | 782 | AMAZIAH |
| JEHOASH | | 784 | |
| | | 790 | |

| KINGS OF ISRAEL | PROPHETS OF ISRAEL | KINGS OF JUDAH | PROPHETS OF JUDAH |
|---|---|---|---|
| **NORTHERN KINGDOM (ISRAEL)** | | **SOUTHERN KINGDOM (JUDAH)** | |

### 5. *Place in the canon*

We observed in Lesson 1 that Hosea heads the canonical list of the twelve minor prophets. Review the lesson's brief discussion of this.

## II. SURVEY

Recall how you made surveys of the books of Jonah and Amos. We will follow the same procedures here. Our goal is to see the general, overall structure of the book and some of its highlights.

1. Scan chapters 1-3. Who are some of the main characters of this narrative? Do not tarry at this time over questions that come to mind concerning the Lord's instructions to Hosea.

2. Study the survey Chart S. Observe that there are two main divisions in the book. How do chapters 4-14 differ from 1-3 as to type of content? Scan chapters 4-14 to verify this.

3. Spend the next hour or so making a casual reading of chapters 4-14. When a verse describes the sin or guilt of God's people, mark *S* in the margin of your Bible. Keep scanning until the subject changes to judgment (*J*), invitation (*I*), restoration (*R*), or grace (*G*). When there is a change of subject, record the new letter at that point. When you have done this for all the chapters, you will note that all the subjects mentioned above appear scattered throughout the section. In other words, a clear outline is not evident. However, observe on Chart S what subjects seem prominent in chapters 4-8, 9-10, and 11-14. Compare this outline with the markings you have just made. For example, is judgment more prominent than sin in chapters 9-10?

4. How do chapters 4-14 reflect Hosea's experiences in chapters 1-3, according to Chart S?

5. The last chapter of Hosea (chap. 14) is a key Bible passage on the cure for spiritual backsliding. How does the chapter serve as a conclusion to Hosea's book? Who is the prominent person of the last sentence of the book?

6. Note the list of key words on the chart. Add to this list as you continue your study of the book.

7. Note also the key verses cited on the chart. Read the verses in your Bible. Relate them to the theme of the book. What title for the book is shown on the chart? Try arriving at a title of your own.

\* \* \*

## REVIEW QUESTIONS

1. What does the name *Hosea* mean literally?

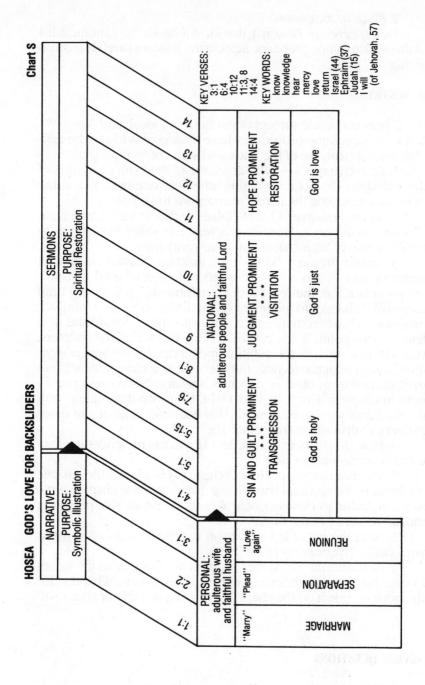

# HOSEA  GOD'S LOVE FOR BACKSLIDERS

Chart S

| | NARRATIVE | SERMONS |
|---|---|---|
| | PURPOSE: Symbolic Illustration | PURPOSE: Spiritual Restoration |

| | 1:1 | 2:2 | 3:1 | 4:1 | 5:1 | 5:15 | 7:6 | 8:1 | 9 | 10 | 11 | 12 | 13 | 14 |
|---|---|---|---|---|---|---|---|---|---|---|---|---|---|---|

PERSONAL: adulterous wife and faithful husband

| "Marry" | "Plead" | "Love again" |
|---|---|---|
| MARRIAGE | SEPARATION | REUNION |

NATIONAL: adulterous people and faithful Lord

| SIN AND GUILT PROMINENT *** | JUDGMENT PROMINENT *** | HOPE PROMINENT *** |
|---|---|---|
| TRANSGRESSION | VISITATION | RESTORATION |
| God is holy | God is just | God is love |

KEY VERSES:
3:1
6:4
10:12
11:3, 8
14:4

KEY WORDS:
know
knowledge
hear
mercy
love
return
Israel (44)
Ephraim (37)
Judah (15)
I will
(of Jehovah, 57)

84

2. What is known about Hosea's home life?

3. What people were mainly Hosea's audience?

4. Name some of the kings and prophets who were Hosea's contemporaries.

5. When may Hosea have finished writing his book?

6. Describe the political, economic, and spiritual conditions of Israel in Hosea's time.

7. What is the main theme of the book of Hosea?

8. Compare Hosea with Jeremiah and with Amos.

9. Compare chapters 1-3 with 4-14. How much of the survey chart can you recall?

10. List some of the key words of Hosea. Can you quote a key verse of the book?

# Lesson 10

# Hosea and His Unfaithful Wife

God let Hosea experience desertion by his wife to show how Israel's spiritual adultery grieved Him. The trauma of marrying a woman who turned out to be a prostitute must have been anguish for Hosea. But it made him a better prophet, for it was a trial from the hand of God. When he preached God's words to Israel, "Ye are not my people," he had understanding of the agony of God's heart.

This present lesson is about the first few years of Hosea's marriage to Gomer.

## I. PREPARATION FOR STUDY

1. Before analyzing chapters 1-3 you will want to consider the various views held about Hosea's marriage to Gomer and, if possible, arrive at your own conclusions. First, read 1:2. What problem presents itself, concerning what Hosea was commanded to do?

You will first want to choose between the allegorical and historical interpretations of this marriage:

*Allegorical*: The marriage and birth of children are allegory or parable (or dream, vision) intended to portray truths about Israel and God *figuratively*.

*Historical*: The narrative is *factual*, intended to *illustrate* truths about Israel and God by way of symbols. The strong argument in favor of this view is that the Bible text reads *naturally* as historical narrative.[1] This is the view followed by this manual.

After you have chosen one of the above interpretations, you will need to choose one of these four options concerning the story:

---

1. Compare similar narratives in Jer. 13 and Ezek. 4.

(a) When Hosea married Gomer, he knew she was already a harlot.

(b) When Hosea married Gomer, only God knew that she was already a harlot.

(c) When Hosea married Gomer, he knew that she would later become a harlot.

(d) When Hosea married Gomer, only God knew that she would later become a harlot.

The first two options (a) and (b) are least likely, since they do not symbolize what was true about Israel's original relationship to God, namely, faithfulness. In this connection read Jeremiah 3:6-14 and note the three stages of Israel's relationship to God:

(1) Israel is originally faithful (cf. Hos. 9:10).

(2) Backslidden Israel commits spiritual adultery.

(3) Israel is restored.

You may want to study this subject further in a commentary.[2]

2. Read 2 Kings 9:1–10:11 for background to Hosea 1:4.

3. Record on paper these literal meanings of the Hebrew names appearing in Hosea 1:

| | |
|---|---|
| Jezreel: | "God sows" or "God scatters" |
| Lo-ruhamah: | "unloved" or "not pitied" |
| Lo-ammi: | "not my people" |

(Note: the prefix *lo* is the Hebrew negative.)

4. Throughout the book of Hosea there are prophecies of future judgment and future restoration of Israel. When you try to identify when in history the prophecies are fulfilled, keep in mind the principle of double reference in Bible prophecy studied in Lesson 8. Review Chart Q, which shows two main judgments and two main restorations. When Hosea prophesied future judgment for Israel, both near and distant fulfillments may have been in view (double-reference principle). The same is true of prophesied restorations. Apply this principle as you study Hosea's book.

## II. ANALYSIS

*Segment to be analyzed*: 1:1–2:1
*Paragraph divisions*: at verses 1:1, 2, 3*b*, 6, 8, 10

### A. Introductory Verse: 1:1

What does this verse contribute to the message of the book? Locate on Chart R the kings mentioned in this verse. Why do you

---

2. See Hobart E. Freeman, *An Introduction to the Old Testament Prophets*, pp. 178-82, for a good discussion of the various views.

1:2

PRESENT
—CONDITION

3b

FUTURE
—CONSEQUENCES

Jezreel:

6

Lo-Ruhamah:

8

Lo-Ammi:

10

ULTIMATE
—HOPE

Ammi:

Ruhamah:

2:1

think Hosea lists all the kings of Judah who reigned during his ministry but omits the six kings of Israel after Jeroboam? (Various answers are suggested by commentaries.)

### B. Israel's Adultery: 1:2–2:1

Chart T is a work sheet for recording observations as you analyze this passage.
1. What was Israel's spiritual condition when Hosea wrote (1:2)?

_____

_____

2. What three judgments are prophesied symbolically in the three middle paragraphs?

_____

_____

_____

Do you see a progression here?

_____

3. What is prophesied about Israel in verse 4?

_____

When did the kingdom "cease"?

_____

4. What is the first word of the last paragraph?

_____

What does it suggest?

_____

How far into the future does the prophecy of this last paragraph point? Read Romans 9:25-26 and 1 Peter 2:10.

_____

5. Compare God's sowings ("Jezreel") of 1:11 and 1:4.

_____

6. The words "Say ye" of 2:1 may be addressed to the godly remnant of 1:10-11. Then 2:1 is an appropriate conclusion to the paragraph about ultimate restoration (1:10–2:1). What do the names *Ammi* and *Ruhamah* mean?

_____

7. As you look back over this opening chapter of Hosea, recall the threefold progression:

|                    |              |
|--------------------|--------------|
| TRANSGRESSION      | (present)    |
| JUDGMENT           | (future)     |
| RESTORATION        | (ultimate)   |

(The restoration involves only a believing remnant.) This three-fold message of Hosea will appear over and over again in his book.

## III. NOTES

1. *"I will have mercy upon the house of Judah"* (1:7). In 722 B.C. Israel fell to the Assyrian invaders, but when Sennacherib came down to besiege Jerusalem, God defended the city. Read 2 Kings 19:35-36.

2. *"Judah and . . . Israel be gathered together"* (1:11). Compare Jeremiah 3:18 for a similar prophecy.

3. *"Day of Jezreel"* (1:11). Merrill Unger comments: "'The [great] day of Jezreel' will be Armageddon's slaughter, a prelude to the destruction of Israel's last-day enemies, and restoration."[3] Others see in the phrase "day of Jezreel" a glorious sowing: "After the people of Israel had been scattered because of their sin, God would plant or 'sow' them in their own land again."[4] Compare 2:23. Also read 1:11 in *The Living Bible* for a similar interpretation.

## IV. FOR THOUGHT AND DISCUSSION

1. How is marriage a figurative representation of the Christian's relation to Christ? (Cf. Eph. 5:30-32; John 14:3; Rev. 19:7-9.) What can mar this intimate relationship, bringing on spiritual adultery? (Cf. James 4:4.)

2. Can a backslidden Christian be restored to fellowship with Christ? If so, how is such restoration brought about? (Cf. Rev. 2:4-5.)

3. Relate Hosea 1:4 to these verses about the vengeance of God: Romans 3:5; 12:19; Hebrews 10:30.

4. How do you reconcile these two prophecies about Israel:
"I will no more have mercy upon the house of Israel" (1:6).
"It shall be said unto them [Israel], Ye are the sons of the living God" (1:10).

5. What does chapter 1 teach about God?

---

3. Merrill F. Unger, *Unger's Bible Handbook*, p. 399.
4. Charles F. Pfeiffer, "Hosea," in *The Wycliffe Bible Commentary*, p. 803.

## V. FURTHER STUDY

1. Study the subject of spiritual backsliding in both the Old and New Testaments.
2. You may want to look further into the analytical method of study that organizes observations on a chart similar to Chart T. This method is described in detail in my book *Independent Bible Study.*

## VI. WORDS TO PONDER

Where it is said to them, "You are not My people," it will be said to them, "You are the sons of the living God" (Hos. 1:10*b*, NASB).

# Hosea and Wife Reunited

The two chapters of this lesson tell the sequel of the Hosea-Gomer story of shame and tragedy. The narrative, as applied to Israel, ends "in the latter days," on the bright note of Israel's returning, seeking, and fearing the Lord (3:5). Someone has said, "God hid a gospel in the heart of Hosea's sufferings." That gospel shines forth in all of its splendor in the passage of this lesson.

## I. PREPARATION FOR STUDY

1. First review Chart S to note how chapters 1-3 introduce the longer section of chapters 4-14.

2. Next learn how chapters 1, 2, and 3 are related. Chart U shows some of these relationships. Keeping in mind the action of chapter 1 studied in the previous lesson, scan chapters 2 and 3. Note the following, as shown on Chart U:

(a) There is a progression from marriage to separation to reunion. This manual follows the view that the adulteress of 3:1 is Gomer.

(b) The opening commands to marry, plead, and love introduce the main theme of each of the chapters. (*Who* speaks *to whom*, in each case? Read the Bible text.)

(c) Which chapter records more descriptions than actions?

(d) Note that each chapter ends on the bright note of ultimate restoration of a godly remnant of Israel. Mark in your Bible the verse that begins this concluding note in each chapter.

## II. ANALYSIS

*Segment to be analyzed*: 2:2-23 and 3:1-5
*Paragraph divisions*: at verses 2:2, 6, 14; 3:1, 4, 5. Mark the paragraph divisions in your Bible.

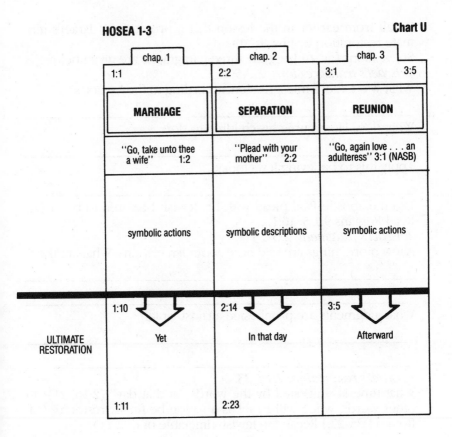

### A. Separation: 2:2-23

This segment is titled "Separation" because such is the setting of the opening paragraphs. What phrases in verse 2 state this clearly?

_____

_____

Who speaks these words?

_____

Whom does he represent, figuratively?

_____

Scan the next verses and note that eventually, at verse 13, the figurative merges with the literal, in the words "saith the Lord." (See also vv. 16 and 21.) Who does Gomer represent, figuratively?

_____

93

Recall from earlier in the lesson that a prophecy of Israel's ultimate restoration begins at 2:14.

Suggestions for studying the three paragraphs are given below.

1. *Israel's transgressions: 2:2-5*

What was Israel's transgression, according to these verses?

_____

What does Hosea urge his children to do?

_____

Apply this to believing Jews today.

_____

Did the apostle Paul plead with his Jewish brethren to be saved? Read Romans 9:1-5; 10:1-2.

2. *Israel's judgment: 2:6-13*

A few more things are said here about Israel's sins. What are they?

_____

_____

What judgments are prophesied against Israel?

_____

_____

3. *Israel's restoration: 2:14-23*

What time is suggested by the words "at that day" (2:16, 21)? In other words, when will Israel as a nation be finally restored? (Cf. Rom. 11:25-27.) Recall the Jewish timetable of Chart Q.

_____

_____

Compare 2:16 and 2:2, with this in mind: *Ishi* means "my husband"; *Baali* means "my Baal-master."

_____

Tarry over verses 19-20. When will Israel enter into this relationship with the Lord?

_____

Note how the three names of Hosea's children appear at the end of the passage:

    Jezreel      — in verse 22; also it is suggested by the phrase "I will sow her," in verse 23

    Lo-ruhamah — in verse 23: "her that had not obtained mercy"

    Lo-ammi    — in verse 23: "not my people"

## B. Reunion: 3:1-5

Chapter 3 is a beautiful illustration of the grace and mercy of God. The domestic story of chapter 1 is tragic, though not uncommon. The story of chapter 3 is something else. Morgan writes:

> But the story of a man seeking a woman when she has passed through all the period of passion, and has lost her value on the material level, and is merely a slave; and of such a man going after her, buying her for thirty shekels and bringing her back, and restoring her to his side as his bride, is something very uncommon.[1]

The chapter is as glorious as it is brief. There would be no gospel of salvation were it not for the grace of God as illustrated by this narrative.

Answer the following questions on the basis of the Bible text. (Begin with the assumption that the "woman" of v. 1 is Gomer. The phrase "yet an adulteress" supports this view.)

1. What is suggested by the words "Go, again love" (3:1, NASB)?

_____

_____

2. How do the following words of verse 1 represent the theme of Hosea: "again love ... even as the Lord loves the sons of Israel" (NASB)?

_____

_____

3. How do the last words of verse 1 describe spiritual adultery?

_____

_____

4. How does verse 2 remind you of Christ's work? (Cf. Ex. 21:32; 1 Cor. 6:20; 1 Pet. 1:18-19.)

_____

_____

5. Verse 3 teaches a reunion of Hosea and Gomer but with temporary restrictions placed on Gomer. For a period of time Gomer, living in virtual seclusion, would "not be for man."[2] That is, she would be deprived of marital relations with Hosea until fully re-

1. G. Campbell Morgan, *Hosea*, p. 8.
2. The word "another" was not in the original autographs.

95

stored.[3] Verse 4 is seen as the fulfillment of this in Israel's experience during exile. In what sense was Israel deprived of the things mentioned in verse 4 during exile?

6. Verse 5 prophesies about restored Israel. What words and phrases of the verse indicate that the messianic kingdom of the end times is meant, not primarily the return from Babylonian captivity in the sixth century B.C.

## III. NOTES

1. *"Which they prepared for Baal"* (2:8). The *New Berkeley Version* reads, "Which they made into a Baal." *The Living Bible* paraphrases, "That she used in worshiping Baal, her god."
2. *"Valley of Achor"* (2:15). The Hebrew word *akhor* means "trouble" or "troubling." The valley was originally named this because of the trouble brought on by sin. (Read Josh. 7:1, 20-21, 25-26.) But through God's grace the valley of trouble is transformed into a door of hope (2:15; cf. Isa. 65:10).
3. *"Flagons of wine"* (3:1). Most versions translate this as "cakes of raisins." One of the pagan Baal rites was to offer cakes of dried grapes.
4. *"David their king"* (3:5). When Hosea wrote this, David, father of Solomon, had been dead 250 years. This is clearly a reference to Christ, the messianic David. (Cf. Ezek. 34:23-24; 37:24-25.)

## IV. FOR THOUGHT AND DISCUSSION

1. What is temporary about the pleasures and allurements of the world? See 2:7*a*. Also read Hebrews 11:24-26.
2. Why is it important for Christians to acknowledge continually God's gracious provisions for all their needs? Is it possible that ingratitude is a cause as well as a symptom of backsliding? See 2:8.
3. How do the words "she . . . forgat me" (2:13) describe a backslidden believer?
4. Would you find it difficult to truly love someone who has deserted or harmed you? What does 3:1 teach about God's love for His people?
5. If you are studying in a group, let the members recount some of the impressions that the first three chapters have made

3. See *The Wycliffe Bible Commentary*, p. 805.

on them. You may want to reflect on the teaching about God, suggested by the following summary:[4]
    (a) God suffers when His people are unfaithful.
    (b) God cannot tolerate or condone sin.
    (c) God loves the sinner in spite of his sin.
    (d) God seeks to restore the sinner.

## V. FURTHER STUDY

Study what the Bible teaches about a *new covenant* ("In that day will I make a covenant for them," 2:18). Here are some key passages to read: Jeremiah 31:31-34; Hebrews 8:8-13; 12:22-24.

## VI. WORDS TO PONDER

They [Israel] will return to the Lord their God, and to the Messiah, their King, and they shall come trembling, submissive to the Lord and to his blessings in the end times (Hos. 3:5, *The Living Bible*).

---

4. Summary by Morgan, p. 18.

# Sin Brings Judgment

The remainder of the book of Hosea records messages of the prophet reflecting the theme of chapters 1-3. Actually the messages are predominantly the words of the Lord, quoted by Hosea. The opening line of chapter 4 introduces this: "Hear the word of the Lord, ye children of Israel." We do not know the details of the setting of the messages—for example, how many different sermons they represent, how the Lord's words were transmitted to Hosea for prophetic delivery, and when and where they were spoken. The messages themselves, as they stand compiled in the book, fulfill the purposes of God in His Scriptures, and this is the preeminent factor.

As stated above, chapters 4-14 reflect the theme of chapters 1-3. In fact, the organization of chapters 4-14 follows in a general way the *order* of subjects in chapters 1, 2, and 3. Think back over these latter chapters and see if you agree with the following identifications:

*Chapter 1*: The *transgression* of Israel is prominent here, since the symbol of adultery is the key symbol in the narrative.[1]

*Chapter 2*: The *judgment* of Israel is prominent here, even though a long paragraph of hope is included (2:14-23).

*Chapter 3*: The *restoration* of Israel is clearly the key subject of this narrative.

Now let us relate these to chapters 4-14. You may recall in the earlier survey of the whole book how the general subjects of 4-14 were identified. See Chart S. Chart V shows how chapters 4-14 amplify the subjects of chapters 1-3.

---

1. We have already seen that *judgment* and *restoration* appear in the chapter, but they do not overtake *transgression* as to prominence.

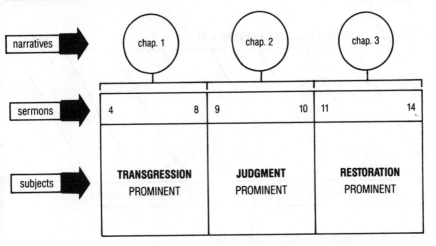

## I. PREPARATION FOR STUDY

1. Refer to the *Notes* for a list of substitute readings intended to clarify the meaning of the King James text. Record these in your Bible at this time.

2. As you study the messages of Hosea in this and the following lesson, do not lose sight of the man Hosea, who pleaded with his brethren with such agony of soul. More than that, be aware that most of the words are spoken by the Lord Himself, who kept on extending more of His grace to favored people who still chose to desert Him.

## II. ANALYSIS

*Segments to be analyzed*: 4:1-19; 5:1-14; 5:15–6:11; 7:1-16; 8:1-14; 9:1-17; 10:1-15

*Paragraph divisions*: at verses 4:1, 4, 7, 11, 15; 5:1, 8, 15; 6:4; 7:1, 8; 8:1, 8, 11; 9:1, 7, 10, 15; 10:1, 3, 11[2] (Mark these in your Bible.)

### A. General Analysis

There is no clear topical outline in chapters 4-8 or 9-10. The best way to approach the passage is chapter by chapter, being aware of the paragraph divisions within each chapter. If in your studies you detect a main theme for a particular chapter, record this in the ob-

---

2. With one exception (5:15), these are the paragraph divisions of NASB.

lique spaces of Chart W. Do not feel frustrated if such themes are hard to identify.[3]

**MAIN THEMES OF CHAPTERS 4-10**　　　　　　　　　　**Chart W**

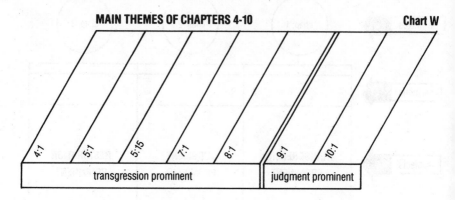

### B. Chapter-by-Chapter Analysis

Now read chapter 4 more slowly than you have done so up to this point. Underline words and phrases that strike you as significant, unique, or important for whatever reason. Record in your own words on the accompanying work sheet some of the sins and judgments appearing in the chapter. If there is any reference to restoration (including invitations to restoration), record this. Follow this procedure for chapters 5-10 also.

### C. Two Topical Studies

1. *Prophecies of Assyrian captivity*
Go through chapters 4-10 looking for references to the imminent Assyrian invasion and captivity. The references may be either specific or only implied.

2. *Two bright passages*
You probably have observed that 6:1-3 and 10:12 are oases in the bleak deserts of Hosea's prophecies. Let the following suggestions be starters of study for you:

(a) *6:1-3.* Some modern versions connect 5:15 with 6:1-3. (See Notes for one example.) Some Bible students interpret 6:1-3 as only a profession of repentance, not from the heart. This is based on the Lord's response of 6:4, where He says their good-

---

3. A less difficult exercise would be to look for paragraph themes rather than chapter themes.

| Chapter | SIN | JUDGMENT | RESTORATION |
|---------|-----|----------|-------------|
| 4 | | | |
| 5 | | | |
| 6 | | | |
| 7 | | | |
| 8 | | | |
| 9 | | | |
| 10 | | | |

ness[4] was only a fleeting thing—"like the dew which goes away early." What are your conclusions? Would the confessions of 6:1-3 be acceptable to the Lord if they came from hearts of genuine repentance?

(b) *10:12*. Read verses 11 and 12 in *The Living Bible*. Does it strike you as significant that the short invitation of 10:12 appears after such a long passage on sin and judgment?

### III. NOTES

1. Some phrases of the King James Version are not clear. The following substitute readings will help you better understand the text.[5]

| Reference | King James Reading | Substitute Reading |
|:---:|:---:|:---:|
| 4:12 | ask counsel at their stocks | consult their wooden idol |
| 4:16 | Now the Lord will | Can the Lord . . . ? |
| 4:18 | with shame do love, Give ye. | dearly love shame. |
| 5:2 | are profound to make slaughter | have gone deep in depravity |
| 5:7 | a month | the new moon |
| 5:10 | remove the bound | move a boundary |
| 5:11 | he willingly walked after the commandment | he was determined to follow man's command |
| 5:15 | they will seek me early. | and then their cry will be: |
| 6:5 | thy judgments | the judgments on you |
| 7:13 | Though I have redeemed them, | I would redeem them, but |
| 10:1 | yet an empty vine | a luxuriant vine[6] |

2. The reference to Ephraim at 4:17 is the first of thirty-seven such references in Hosea. Although Ephraim was just one of the ten tribes of the Northern Kingdom, the name was often used synonymously with Israel, probably because it was the largest and most prestigious of the tribes. (Cf. 13:1, 15*a*, in *Berkeley*.)

### IV. FOR THOUGHT AND DISCUSSION

1. Apply the following phrases to the present day:

4. G. Campbell Morgan suggests "submission" as a correct translation of the Hebrew. NASB reads "loyalty." Read Morgan's commentary *Hosea*, pp. 46-55, for an excellent treatment of this passage.
5. Most of the substitute readings are from the NASB.
6. The vine of Israel was luxuriant, but it was producing degenerate fruit: "fruit for himself," not for God.

"There is no truth, nor mercy, nor knowledge of God" (4:1)
"Like people, like priest" (4:9)
"Israel slideth back as a backsliding heifer" (4:16)
"Ephraim is joined to idols: let him alone" (4:17)
"I desired mercy, and not sacrifice" (6:6)
"Ephraim is a cake not turned" (7:8)
"They have not cried unto me with their heart" (7:14)
"They return, but not to the most High" (7:16)
"Now Israel . . . says, 'Help us, for you are our God!' But it is too late!" (8:2, TLB)
"They have sown the wind, and they shall reap the whirl-wind" (8:7)
"I have written to him the great things of my law" (8:12)
"Israel hath forgotten his Maker" (8:14)
"The days of recompense are come" (9:7)
"My God will cast them away" (9:17)
"They shall be wanderers among the nations" (9:17)
"It is time to seek the Lord" (10:12)

2. God is love *and* holiness. How are these two attributes manifested in the passage of this lesson? Some people stress God's love to the exclusion of His holiness. Others stress His holiness to the exclusion of His love. What is the outcome of each of these extremes in daily living? Do you see any of this in America today?

### V. FURTHER STUDY

1. There are many geographical references in this passage. In most cases there is an Old Testament story associated with the geography. Make a study of the historical backgrounds to see how the geographical references illustrate the spiritual truths.

2. You may want to study the references in this passage to the Southern Kingdom of Judah.

### VI. WORDS TO PONDER

G. Campbell Morgan, on enthusiasm:

> If the things we affirm in our creeds are true, we ought to be on fire. . . . I am not pleading for a simulated enthusiasm. . . . But if we have lost our flame; if we have lost our fire; if we have lost our fury, under certain circumstances, against evil; it is because we have lost our vision of God, and we have lost our sense of the greatness of our evangel.[7]

7. G. Campbell Morgan, *Hosea*, p. 85.

# Lesson 13

Hosea 11:1–14:9

# Hope for Backsliders

The theme of hope and restoration is prominent in the last four chapters of this inspired prophecy. Much of chapters 12 and 13 is about Israel's sin and judgment, but this accentuates the long-suffering mercies of God described in the surrounding chapters, 11 and 14. For example, chapter 14 is the Bible's classic chapter on God's love extended to backsliders. Here is how one writer describes the chapters studied in this lesson:

> Light breaks over these last chapters. They give us a picture of Israel's ultimate blessings in the future kingdom. We get a glimpse into God's heart of love when He, as a father, says, When Israel was a child, then I loved him and called my son out of Egypt. (Hos. 11:1)[1]

## I. PREPARATION FOR STUDY

1. Review Chart S and observe how chapters 11-14 complete the three-part theme of Hosea's prophecy.

2. Mark in your Bible the paragraph divisions shown below. This will help you organize your studies as you move among the chapters.

| Reference | King James Reading | Substitute Reading |
|-----------|--------------------|--------------------|
| 11:2 | As they called them, so they went from them | the more I called to them, the more they deserted Me |
| 11:11 | they shall tremble | they shall come trembling |
| 12:8 | In all my labours they shall find none iniquity in me that were sin | In all my labors they will find in me no iniquity, which would be sin. |

1.  Henrietta C. Mears, *What the Bible Is All About*, pp. 280-81.

104

3. Use the preceding substitute readings in the Bible text:

## II. ANALYSIS

*Segments to be analyzed*: 11:1-11; 11:12–13:16; 14:1-8; 14:9
*Paragraph divisions*: at verses 11:1, 5, 8, 12; 12:2, 7, 12; 13:2, 4, 9, 12, 15; 14:1, 4, 8, 9

### A. General Analysis

Chart X divides this passage into three main sections (plus the concluding verse, 14:9). The theme of chapter 14 is identified on the chart by the word *restoration*. Scan the chapters of the other two sections and try to identify themes for these as well. Record your conclusions on the chart.

**HOSEA 11-14**                                                              **Chart X**

| Lord | Hosea | Lord | Hosea | Lord | Hosea | Lord | Hosea |

11:1 11:5 11:8 11:12 12:2 12:7 12:12 13:2 13:4 13:9 13:12 13:15 14:1 14:4 14:8 14:9

14:1 call to repentance
14:4 promise of pardon

RESTORATION | CONCLUSION

At some places in the chapters the prophet Hosea appears to inject his own thoughts before continuing with more direct words of the Lord. The speakers, whether Hosea or the Lord, are identified at the top of Chart X.[2] Mark the Hosea sections in your Bible.

### B. Segment Analysis

1. *The Lord's compassion: 11:1-11*
Compare 11:1-4 with 11:8-11.

---

2. See Morgan, *Hosea*, p. 98, for these suggested assignments of the Hosea sections. The paragraph divisions noted earlier coincide with these sections.

What are the two different time references?

_____

How is the intervening paragraph (11:5-7) a contrasting one?

_____

In the oblique spaces on Chart X, record a main subject for each of the three paragraphs.

2. *Israel's sin and judgment: 11:12–13:16*

Read the segment paragraph by paragraph and record a main subject in each oblique space on Chart X. You may want to record on a separate piece of paper what this passage teaches about the following:

    Israel's sin
    Israel's judgments
    God's past mercies
    God's present invitations
    God's promises of restorations

3. *Restoration of the backslider: 14:1-8*

What conditions must be met for a backslider's restoration, according to 14:1-3?

_____

_____

How do verses 4-7 describe the restoration?

_____

_____

See the *New American Standard Bible* or *The Living Bible* for a clearer reading of 14:8.[3]

4. *Conclusion: 14:9*

How does this verse serve as a conclusion or epilogue of the book of Hosea?

_____

Does it surprise you that a direct reference to God's love is lacking? Compare this concluding verse with 1:2, which introduced the setting of the book.

_____

_____

3. See *The Wycliffe Bible Commentary*, p. 817, for the view that the various lines of v. 8 are a dialogue between Israel and God.

## III. FOR THOUGHT AND DISCUSSION

1. Is man's responsibility proportional to the light that God gives him? Read Hosea 12:10; Romans 1:19-23; Luke 12:47-48.

2. Is the security of a nation ultimately dependent on military might? See 14:3*a*. On the phrase "we will not ride upon horses," compare Isaiah 30:16; 31:1.

3. What does Hosea 14 prophesy about the future of Israel? Read Romans 11 to learn what Paul taught about Israel as a nation. Was there a remnant of believing Jews in Paul's day (11:5)? How far into the future was Paul looking when he wrote 11:25-26?

4. Compare the love of God in the book of Hosea with His love manifested in the New Testament gospel. Relate to this the words of the apostle Paul,

> The proof of God's amazing love is this: that it was WHILE WE WERE SINNERS that Christ died for us. (Rom. 5:7-8, Phillips; emphasis added)

## SUMMARY

Below are given parts of two key verses for each of the three minor prophets studied in this manual. Let them serve as reminders of some of the grand truths taught about God in the books.

JONAH: "Salvation is of the Lord" (Jonah 2:9)
           "Should not I spare Nineveh?" (Jonah 4:11)
AMOS: "The Lord will roar from Zion" (Amos 1:2)
           "Seek ye me, and ye shall live" (Amos 5:4)
HOSEA: "How shall I give thee up, Ephraim?" (Hos. 11:8)
           "I will heal their backsliding" (Hos. 14:4)

# Bibliography

## RESOURCES FOR FURTHER STUDY

Archer, Gleason L. *A Survey of Old Testament Introduction*. Chicago: Moody, 1964.

Douglas, J. D., ed. *The New Bible Dictionary*. Grand Rapids: Eerdmans, 1962.

Jensen, Irving L. *Independent Bible Study*. Chicago: Moody, 1963.

————. *Jensen's Survey of the Old Testament*. Chicago: Moody, 1978.

*The New International Version Study Bible*. Grand Rapids: Zondervan, 1985.

*The Ryrie Study Bible*. Chicago: Moody, 1985.

Schultz, Arnold C. *The Prophets Speak*. New York: Harper, 1968.

Strong, James. *The Exhaustive Concordance of the Bible*. New York: Abingdon, 1890.

Tenney, Merrill C., ed. *The Zondervan Pictorial Bible Dictionary*. Grand Rapids: Zondervan, 1963.

*The Thompson Chain Reference Bible*. Indianapolis: Kirkbride, 1934.

Unger, Merrill F. *The New Unger's Bible Handbook*. Chicago: Moody, 1984.

Whitcomb, John C. *Old Testament Kings and Prophets*. Rev. ed. Chart. Chicago: Moody, 1968.

Young, Edward J. *An Introduction to the Old Testament*. Grand Rapids: Eerdmans, 1949.

Young, Robert. *Analytical Concordance to the Bible*. Grand Rapids: Eerdmans, n.d.

## COMMENTARIES AND TOPICAL STUDIES

Banks, William L. *Jonah: The Reluctant Prophet.* Chicago: Moody, 1966.

Ellison, H. L. "I and II Kings." In *The New Bible Commentary*, ed. F. Davidson; Stibbs, A. M.; and Kevan, E. F. Grand Rapids: Eerdmans, 1953.

Fairbairn, Patrick. *Jonah: His Life, Character, and Mission.* Grand Rapids: Kregel, 1964.

Gaebelein, Frank E. *Four Minor Prophets.* Chicago: Moody, 1970.

Morgan, G. Campbell. *Hosea: The Heart and Holiness of God.* Westwood, N.J.: Revell, 1934.

Pfeiffer, Charles F. "Hosea." In *The Wycliffe Bible Commentary*. Edited by Charles F. Pfeiffer and Everett F. Harrison. Chicago: Moody, 1962.

Robinson, D. "Jonah." In *The New Bible Commentary*, ed. F. Davidson; Stibbs, A. M.; and Kevan, E. F. Grand Rapids: Eerdmans, 1953.

Robinson, George L. *The Twelve Minor Prophets.* Grand Rapids: Baker, 1952.

Schultz, Arnold C. "Amos." In *The Wycliffe Bible Commentary*. Edited by Charles F. Pfeiffer and Everett F. Harrison. Chicago: Moody, 1962.

Moody Press, a ministry of the Moody Bible Institute,
is designed for education, evangelization, and edification.
If we may assist you in knowing more about Christ
and the Christian life, please write us without obligation:
Moody Press, c/o MLM, Chicago, Illinois 60610.